# LAGUNA BEACH
### THE REAL ORANGE COUNTY

# *LAGUNA BEACH*

### THE REAL ORANGE COUNTY

# Life Inside the Bubble

## KATHY PASSERO
## AND BETH EFRAN

NEW YORK   LONDON   TORONTO   SYDNEY

POCKET BOOKS, a division of Simon & Schuster, Inc.
1230 Avenue of the Americas, New York, NY 10020

ISBN-13: 978-1-4165-2030-6
ISBN-10:    1-4165-2030-9

This MTV Books/Pocket Books trade paperback edition November 2005

10   9   8   7   6   5   4   3   2   1

Manufactured in the United States of America

For information regarding special discounts for bulk purchases,
please contact Simon & Schuster Special Sales at 1-800-456-6798
or business@simonandschuster.com

LAGUNA BEACH
THE REAL ORANGE COUNTY

# INTRODUCTION

Welcome to Laguna Beach. Brace yourself for hookups and heartbreak, cliques and crushes, parties, players, drama queens, hot guys, and mean girls. Gossip spreads like wildfire, and the seniors rule the school.

And don't forget the money—outrageous amounts of it. Or the beach—if you live in Laguna, you *live* at the beach. Thank God Louis Vuitton purses look awesome with Roxy board shorts.

Despite all this fabulousness, Laguna Beach still feels like a small town. Sometimes it feels way *too* small. By senior year, everybody knows all the details of your personal life and your past, no matter how embarrassing—and some of it is *horribly embarrassing*. Even the early years of the guys and girls of Laguna Beach were filled with heartbreak, gossip, and drama. . . .

# LAUREN, STEPHEN, AND KRISTIN

## The Showdown at the St. Regis

As Lauren got dressed and put on her makeup to get ready for her friend Jen's birthday party at the St. Regis, in the fall of their senior year, she mulled over the Stephen situation. Things were weird, but hopefully she'd finally gotten them under control.

After the night she'd kissed Cache, a junior, in front of him (big mistake; what was she even thinking?), things had looked hopeless with Stephen. But then Stephen went on vacation and when he got back he forgave her.

Things were really good between them for several weeks. But then these annoying little rumors started flying around. So-and-so had seen Stephen hooking up with Kristin, his old girlfriend, behind her back at such-and-such a place. So-and-so was pretty sure they were getting back together. A few of her friends had gone so far as to tell her, "They're back together. You should forget about him. You two are better off being friends."

Did everyone in Laguna Beach have to know every detail of your personal life and give you advice about it? Why did they all seem to think they knew what was best for you better than you knew it yourself?

That afternoon Lauren had confronted Stephen. "Are you with Kristin again?"

"No, no, no. Who told you that?" he said. "I swear, I have *not* hooked up with Kristin."

Even if he was new in the boyfriend department, Stephen was one of her oldest guy friends. He would never lie to her. Or cheat on her. Would he? Besides, lately he seemed like he was more serious about the relationship than she was.

On the other hand, why would rumors about Kristin keep popping up if there was no truth behind them?

When Lauren walked into Jen's party there was no sign of Stephen. She hung out with Talan for a while, then spotted Kristin on the other side of the room.

To say the two of them had never been best friends was an understatement. Still, Kristin was the one person who could answer the question she was dying to ask. And there would never be a better time than now to ask her.

"Can I talk to you for a minute?"

Kristin looked up, surprised.

Lauren didn't know a delicate way to phrase it, so she just asked point blank if Kristin had been hooking up with Stephen.

"Yes," Kristin said. She couldn't believe Lauren was asking her this. For a month now Stephen had been assuring her that it was over with Lauren. He just wanted to ease out of things slowly, he said, to avoid breaking Lauren's heart. Kristin had been patient against her better judgment, because Lauren and Stephen had known each other forever. She knew he'd be devastated to lose her friendship. Now Kristin was furious.

"He told me things were over between *you two!*" Kristin told Lauren.

"He told me the same thing about you!" Lauren said, her voice rising.

Just about then Stephen walked in. They didn't give the guy a chance to take off his coat. Both Lauren and Kristin cornered him, yanked him into an empty room, and demanded to know the real story.

Soon the three of them were screaming at one another at the top of their lungs. Separate room or not, the whole party was in on the fight. There was no doubt tonight that everybody knew every detail of Kristin, Stephen, and Lauren's personal lives.

"All right," Stephen admitted. "I am hooking up with both of you! But . . ." He paused and turned to face Lauren. "I don't like you, Lauren. I like Kristin."

Lauren felt like someone had punched her in the stomach. It seemed like all the music and conversation had drained away on the other side of the door. Was everybody out there waiting to see what she'd do next? She couldn't bring herself to look at Kristin or Stephen. She couldn't bear to see Kristin's smug smile or Stephen's pathetic I'm-sorry-don't-hate-me look.

Why hadn't she listened to her friends' advice about him?

She turned and ran out of the room, tears already welling up in her eyes. "Sorry," she mumbled as she brushed past Talan on the way out into the hall. She sat down on the floor and cried. And cried.

She was still crying when Stephen walked up and sat down next to her.

"I'm sorry," he said. "I didn't know how to tell you. I didn't want to hurt your feelings."

"Oh, and this way was better?" she snapped sarcastically. "You should've just told me what was going on."

"I still want to be your friend," he ventured.

"I don't want to be *your* friend!" Lauren shouted at him.

But no matter how much she wanted to hate him, Stephen *was* her friend. He always had been. Maybe they were better off that way. Maybe hooking up had been a mistake in the first place.

Finally, Stephen convinced Lauren to go back to the party. She was almost too embarrassed to show her face again, but she tried to make the best of it.

She and Stephen *were* better as friends, she assured herself, wiping away the last of her tears. Besides, there were a lot of other hot guys around. Maybe it wouldn't turn out to be such a bad night after all.

Lauren spotted Talan standing across the room. She did a quick, covert makeup check in a nearby mirror. No streaks of mascara running down her cheeks. No smeared eyeliner.

She strolled up to him.

"Hey, Talan," she said casually. "What's up?"

"Oh no," he said, taking a step backward. "Don't even try, Lauren. I know what you're doing. It's a bad idea. Not tonight."

Lauren sighed in exasperation. She could deal with having everybody know the details of her personal life. It was just part of growing up in the Bubble. But did they really have to know what was best for you better than you knew it yourself?

And if you thought the good stuff didn't start until high school, think again. Like we said, there's *always* been drama in Laguna Beach. Read on and see for yourself . . .

# STEPHEN AND LO

*Heartbreak in the Hallway*

"Go for it, man," one of Stephen's friends urged, nudging him down the hallway toward Lo. "I totally think she might say yes."

Stephen ventured a glance in Lo's direction. She was chatting away outside her classroom, surrounded by a cluster of friends. She seemed completely oblivious to the fact that he was staring at her.

He swallowed hard. At age 11, he was still new to this dating thing, and the thought of asking a girl to go out with him was terrifying. It didn't help that you always had to do it in the hallway of junior high school surrounded by her friends, your friends, and what seemed like the entire sixth grade.

He felt someone's hands against his back, pushing him forward. "The bell's about to ring," one of his friends whispered. "You gotta do it *now!*"

The next thing Stephen knew, he was standing in front of

Lo. Suddenly, he forgot what he was supposed to say. He just stood there. Out of the corners of both eyes he could see her friends peering at him curiously, expectantly. He had to say something, didn't he?

Lo raised her eyebrows. "Yes?" she asked politely.

"Willyougooutwithme??" It came spilling out in a jumble.

"What?"

"Will you go out with me?"

"Oh," she said, taken aback. "Um. Thanks. But, no. I don't think so."

# Stephen and Lauren

## Golf, Otherwise Known As the Dating Kiss of Death

After being shot down by Lo in the school hallway last year, twelve-year-old Stephen was more cautious. He was dying to ask Lauren to go out with him, but he didn't want to risk another public humiliation. So he had come up with a new strategy: He would wait until she was alone. Then he'd spring the question.

But catching a seventh grade girl alone is no easy task. Everywhere Lauren went she seemed to be flanked by friends. If he waited until the coast was clear, he'd be waiting forever.

When he saw her dressed as Superman at school on Halloween, he decided she looked too cute to wait any longer. He tried to block the memory of Lo out of his mind as he hurried over to Lauren before lunch. He ignored her giggling friends, took a deep breath, and blurted it out. "Will you go out with me?"

Lauren smiled. She'd known Stephen for years. They even went to the same church. And he was pretty cute, despite being so skinny and having that bowl haircut.

"Sure," she said. "Okay."

Stephen beamed and breathed a sigh of relief.

"You will?" he said eagerly. "Great."

There was a moment of awkward silence.

"Um . . . okay then. Well, see ya later."

"Yeah. See ya later."

As she headed off to lunch with her friends, Lauren couldn't keep the grin off her face. How things had changed. Just a year ago, she'd been a total dork with braces and friends who were way too into *The Lord of the Rings*. Back then the guys weren't  interested unless you were one of the Foxy Roxies, as Lo and her gang of girls called themselves for the Roxy clothes they wore every day. Lauren, who was on a strict budget imposed by her mom and didn't own a shred of Roxy clothing, couldn't stand Lo. What kind of a girl would call herself a Foxy Roxy anyway? (Neither girl dreamed that a few short years later, when high school started, they would become the best of friends.)

Now Lauren was giving the Foxy Roxies some competition. Just recently a boy named David had tried to kiss her on the cheek in home economics class. "Eeewww!" she'd screamed and pushed him away. She'd had a friend relay the message that she was *not* that kind of girl before the end of the school day.

Still, judging from David and now Stephen, guys were definitely attracted to her.

During the week that Stephen and Lauren went out they talked on the phone every night. Mostly it was dumb stuff about school and friends and which teachers dressed the weirdest or gave the hardest tests. But it was fun anyway.

Stephen thought about his new girlfriend all that Saturday on the golf course. He'd recently discovered the sport thanks to his older brother John and he loved it. He spent hours practicing. The number one item on his Christmas list was a set of clubs.

When he got home from the golf course, Stephen bolted for the shower in the bathroom he shared with John and their sister. It was a well-known fact among the Colletti kids that the hot water lasted just long enough for two consecutive hot showers. Whichever kid got there last was the loser who got stuck taking a cold shower. This time, Stephen won.

Later that evening, he picked up the phone, looking forward to hearing Lauren's voice and seeing her again at school on Monday.

"Oh, hey," she said. "So, what did you do this afternoon?"

Stephen instantly launched into an enthusiastic recap of his day on the course, ending with "it was totally cool!"

There was silence on the other end of the phone.

"Hello?" he said. "Are you still there?"

Across town, Lauren was staring at the walls of her bedroom. She'd recently ripped down the Justin Timberlake posters that once covered them and had taken to painting and repainting the walls in whatever bright color struck her fancy. Right now there were three shades of green on different walls and one white wall covered in stripes. She was trying to picture Stephen standing on a golf course in a funny cap, pants, and a sweater of roughly the same blinding shades of green as her room.

"You . . . you play golf?" she asked hesitantly.

"Sure," he said, puzzled.

"Do you have to wear a hat and plaid pants? No, wait. Do you wear white shoes like the old guys on TV?!" Lauren couldn't help herself. She burst out laughing at the idea of Stephen in a getup like some retired guy in Palm Springs would wear, zooming around on one of those little carts.

"No, no," he said, trying to explain. "It's not like that at all. It's—"

"I'm sorry," Lauren said, cutting him off and wiping away tears of laughter. "I don't think I can go out with you anymore if you play golf."

And that was the end of Stephen/Lauren, round one.

# Stephen and Lo

## Pucker Up, Baby

Ha! thought Stephen as he watched Lo smoothing her costume and reading over her lines. Now I get to kiss you whether you want to or not!

Even after she'd embarrassed him in front of all his friends by refusing to go out with him last year, Stephen still had a crush on Lo. He couldn't help it. He'd gone so far as to draw little hearts all around her picture in his yearbook along with an arrow and a scrawled note reading "She's going to be my wife!"

Now the two of them had landed starring roles in their seventh grade drama class play, *Silver Linings.* One of their many scenes together called for them to kiss. *On the lips.*

Stephen got a little jittery just thinking about it. Sure, a tiny part of him wanted to get revenge by *making* her kiss him. But another, much bigger part was worried about making a good impression. He still wanted her to like him. Or at least to think he was a good kisser.

But there was a problem. Since his kissing experience had been limited to a three-second kiss in fifth grade with his then-girlfriend during a game of truth or dare, he wasn't actually sure that he *was* a good kisser.

He figured the best thing to do would be to lick his lips. He'd make sure they were nice and wet and juicy for her. That's what a good kisser would do . . . wasn't it?

The teacher instructed them to start the scene. Lo said her line. Stephen responded with his. And on it went until the moment when they had to kiss.

Stephen readied himself and moved in.

"Ick!" Lo screamed, wrenching herself away and wiping her mouth on her sleeve.

He heard a few classmates snicker.

"You're not supposed to make your lips all slobbery," Lo told him in disgust. "That's not how you do it! Don't you know how to kiss at all?"

After that Stephen gave up. There was no way he was ever going to impress Lo. He did notice, though, that once he got the hang of things after a few more tries, she didn't seem to mind rehearsing their kissing scene quite so much.

# LAUREN

## The Catch

Lauren was used to being the only girl and the only little kid on the charter fishing boat trips she took with her father. It meant sleeping below deck in a room full of grown fishermen in three-level bunks, like sailors in the navy, but she didn't mind. She loved fishing and she loved spending time with her dad.

Nobody else in the family came along on the trips. Not her mom or her aunts and uncles or even her younger sister. The overnight outings off the California coast were just for Lauren and her father.

They always followed the same routine. Lauren's dad would bait the hook and throw out the line while she watched. Once they had a bite, Dad would work the fish until it got reasonably close to the boat. Then he would hand the rod over to Lauren, who would finish the job by reeling the catch in.

Lauren and her father were lucky when it came to fishing. When she was six she'd caught a tuna almost as big as she was. The charter boat operator snapped a photo of her standing proudly on deck showing off her catch. She had her arm stretched out, the line clutched in one small fist, while the enormous fish dangled next to her, its tail brushing the deck.

The company liked the photo so much they put it on their promotional brochure. Her parents were thrilled. They showed a copy of the pamphlet featuring their daughter the fisherman to everybody who came over to the house to visit.

But one goal kept eluding Lauren when it came to fishing. On every trip, the fishermen would put ten dollars each into a pot. Whoever caught the biggest fish won the jackpot. Lauren wanted more than anything to walk off the boat holding that jackpot.

"We're gonna win it this time," she assured her dad as she leaned against the edge of the boat, watching him bait the hook.

"We sure are," her dad agreed. "This is our lucky day."

Lauren squinted out at the blue waves sparkling in the dazzling sunlight. Somewhere out there was her fish. The winning fish. She smiled, then turned her attention back to the boat. "Dad, that line is too thin," she told him.

"It'll be fine," her dad said, casting the line out into the shimmering water. "Don't worry."

Lauren leaned contentedly against the edge of the boat. Today was definitely their lucky day. Suddenly she saw something tug on the line.

"Dad, you got a bite!"

Her dad was already wrestling with the fishing rod as the line stretched taut and the tip of the rod bowed. Something on the other end was tugging and wriggling frantically.

"It's something big!" Lauren told him, peering out to the point where the line disappeared below the waves. "I really think that line's too thin to hold it."

*Snap!* No sooner had she said the words than the line broke. The reel spun with a disappointing whir and the remaining length of line trailed lazily on the surface of the water. Somewhere below the waves the giant fish, Lauren's winning fish, was swimming away.

Her dad repaired the line, but few interesting bites came their way after that and Lauren turned her attention instead to watching the other fishermen. A man not too far away from where they were standing looked like he was wrestling some enormous sea creature. With a giant splash, Lauren saw the fish burst out of the water. Her heart sank. She knew it would be the winner.

Her dad followed her gaze. "That's okay, Lauren," he said. "There's always next time."

At the end of the trip everybody gathered around to weigh the catches and award the jackpot. Sure enough, the man Lauren had noticed earlier took the honors. As the other fishermen congratulated him, she stepped up for a closer look.

"Hey!" she cried out. "That fish has a second hook in its mouth! Somebody already caught it, but it must have broken the line."

She didn't say anything because nobody would have believed her, but somehow she knew it. That was her fish. The one that got away.

As they headed back to their car, sunburned and tired, salt from the sea air sticking to their skin, Lauren helped her father load the fishing gear and overnight bags into the trunk.

"So, did you have fun?" Lauren's dad asked as they climbed into the car and began the drive home.

"I had a great time. Thanks for taking me fishing, Dad," she said. "But I told you that line was too thin," she couldn't resist adding.

# Lo

## High Pointes

Lo's parents offered to redo her bedroom for her when they moved from Fullerton, California, into their new house in Laguna Beach, but nine-year-old Lo loved the ballet-pink paint that already covered the walls. It was just the right color for an aspiring ballerina. Once her mom helped her add pretty curtains and a few delicate, flowery accents it was the perfect room for any little girl, in Lo's opinion.

In fact, everything about her new house was perfect. It was big enough that Lo and her older sister and younger brother could each have their own rooms. It was surrounded by a big yard with a huge tree, perfect for climbing. And Three Arch Bay, the private gated community where their new house was located, had lots of other kids Lo's age, many of whom soon became her friends.

Best of all, the community had its own private beach. Every weekend Lo's family and their neighbors would line up chairs in the sand so that the adults could spend their afternoons chatting and enjoying the sunshine while the kids swam, surfed, or splashed in the waves. On warm nights, they would all traipse back down to the beach for barbecues and bonfires. Sometimes people even brought takeout pizzas or appetizers they had made to share with their friends from Three Arch.

The only thing that rivaled the beach in Lo's heart was ballet. She took lessons every week at Tyne Dance Academy, along with many of the other little girls from Laguna. For as long as she could remember, Lo's dream had been to get pointe shoes so that she could dance on her toes like the real ballerinas did. She spent countless hours flipping through the big art books on her parents' coffee table, admiring the paintings of dancers in pink ballet slippers with satin ribbons. She wanted to be just like them. Everything about ballerinas seemed graceful and beautiful. She tried again and again to perch on the tips of her toes to practice, grasping a doorknob or chair to balance herself and wishing desperately that she had genuine pointe shoes with hard, molded toes and ribbons that wound around her ankles.

At last when Lo was in seventh grade, her ballet teacher gave the class the news Lo had been waiting for almost all her life. The girls were ready to go *en pointe*. It was all Lo could do to sit still in the car while her mother drove her to a ballet shop in Huntington Beach to buy her very first pair of toe shoes.

The saleswoman took the shoes out of the tissue paper-filled box and handed them to Lo to try on. Lo thought they were the most beautiful shoes she had ever seen. She ran her hand lovingly over each of the pink satin slippers, admiring them, before slipping them on for the first time. She had expected them to make her feet ache, but the gel pads in them made balancing her weight on the tip of her big toe almost comfortable. She looked at herself in the store's mirror, marveling at how the shoes made her look nearly as beautiful and graceful as a real ballerina.

The minute she got home Lo ripped the box open, put on her shoes, and started practicing.

"Lo, what are you doing?" her mother cried when she saw her. "You can't wear those around the house."

"Why not?"

"Your teacher hasn't approved them yet. What if we have to return them? You'll get them all dirty."

Disappointed, Lo dutifully took off her new shoes and placed them tenderly back in the box until later that week when her ballet teacher would give her the go-ahead. Once she did, Lo barely took her shoes off. She practiced all the time. At last she was a real ballerina, just like the ones in the paintings.

It wasn't until almost a month later that Lo came home after ballet class, peeled off her tights, and noticed that one of her toenails was bruised-looking and loose. She barely touched it and it fell off.

"Gross," she said, gingerly touching the raw skin underneath.

As Lo soon discovered, ballet dancers' toenails fall off all the time. They also develop rough, unsightly calluses on their feet from all the hours they spend in pointe shoes.

Lo danced until she was a sophomore in high school. By that point, cute polished toes and visits to the nail salon had become a priority for all the girls, and Lo would often joke that her feet were a pedicurist's nightmare. She still thought going *en pointe* had been worth it for the sense of accomplishment and the sheer joy of dancing. But who would ever have dreamed that underneath that beautiful exterior ballerinas had the ugliest feet in the world?

# STEPHEN AND DIETER

## Tap, Tap, Kiss, Kiss

Stephen and Dieter had developed a system. Since it was impossible to read a junior high school girl's mind and therefore impossible to know when the best time to kiss her would be, you had to have a wingman, and Stephen and Dieter had decided to be each other's.

If Dieter thought the signs looked good with Stephen's date at the movies that afternoon, he would tap his buddy on the shoulder. A tap meant, "Do it now. Kiss her!" In return, Stephen would keep an eye on Dieter's date and do the same for him.

The system was almost foolproof. But, of course, you couldn't let the girl *know* that you had a system. (How hurtin' would you look then?) So the tap had to be subtle. Discreet. Barely perceptible. Stephen and Dieter had practiced so they wouldn't screw it up by being too obvious. They had the system down to a science.

The two 12-year-olds were perfect gentlemen as they headed into the movie theater with their dates. They held the door open. They even sprang for popcorn before leading the ladies to an empty row at the back.

It wasn't too long after the previews ended and the movie began that Dieter felt something on his shoulder. Tap, tap. Tap, tap.

He decided to ignore it.

Tap, tap. Tap, tap!

Dieter squinted at his date in the darkness. He couldn't see her that well but she looked like she was thoroughly enjoying the movie. If he couldn't read her body language sitting right next to her, how could Stephen tell from way over on the other side of him? He shot Stephen a skeptical look.

Stephen raised his eyebrows. "Go for it," he whispered.

Dieter couldn't back down. Not with his wingman sitting there watching. So he made his move. To his amazement, his date didn't seem surprised or offended in the least. She kissed him back.

Boy, he thought, Stephen really knows how to read women.

Dieter tried not to swagger as he escorted his date out of the theater. He hoped Stephen had enjoyed the movie as much as he had. After his own success in the kissing department, he had been too elated to pay much attention to helping out his buddy.

He couldn't do it now, not in front of the girls, but he would definitely have to call Stephen later to thank him. The system had been an excellent idea.

"Okay, well, thanks for going to the movies with me," Dieter said awkwardly when he and the girl reached her house. "I had a really good time."

"Yeah, me too," she said smiling. She gave him a quick kiss good-bye, then headed up the walkway toward her front door.

"Oh, by the way," she said, stopping to turn around. "I totally saw your friend tap you on the shoulder in the movies today. Nice system."

# Stephen and Dieter
## No Recess for the Wicked

"Stephen! Dieter!" The teacher supervising recess at Top of the World Elementary School yelled. "On the yellow line! Now!"

The two friends glanced at each other and grinned. What had they done this time? Was it that last game of tackle football that did them in? Somehow they always managed to break one recess rule or another.

Under the watchful eye of their teacher, the second graders slunk guiltily over to the edge of the playground where a strip of yellow paint ran along the curb. As they drew near it, Stephen stopped suddenly. He nudged Dieter and pointed. Dieter followed his friend's gaze. Then the two of them burst out laughing.

Just ahead, resting neatly on the yellow line, were two pieces of paper. One had the name Stephen written across it. The other said Dieter in capital letters.

Somebody had decided to make it official. The pair of troublemakers spent so many recesses banished to this spot that an anonymous prankster figured they deserved nameplates.

"Very funny," Stephen called to his classmates, waving the piece of paper as he sat down.

Truth be told, neither Stephen nor Dieter minded life on the yellow line. Sitting out recess wasn't bad as long as they got to be together. Besides, class was just as much fun as recess. They sat next to each other, and they managed to break the rules in class as often as they did outside of it.

Their teacher had developed a card system for rule breakers like them. Every kid had a slot with his name written across it on the classroom wall. Inside were four cards, each a different color. Whenever a kid got in trouble, he or she was told to "pull a card." The first card was yellow, a warning. The second was orange, more serious. The third was red, meaning you'd better watch yourself. The fourth and final card was black. It meant "go to the principal's office, *now.*" Stephen and Dieter had pulled more red cards than any other student in their second grade class.

In their opinion, it couldn't be helped. Stephen could hardly sit still in school anyway, and if he got his hands on a can of Coke at lunch, forget it. Dieter's family knew by now to hide the caffeinated soft drinks whenever they heard Stephen's voice in the hallway. And being with Dieter always got Stephen even more wound up.

Today, the two were mock arguing over a girl they both liked. Before long the argument escalated and Stephen, horsing around as usual, bopped the girl over the head with his binder. Problem was, he hit her a little harder than he meant to and she burst into tears.

The teacher was beside herself. "Pull a card!" she ordered. "Both of you!"

Stephen and Dieter already had colorful stacks of cards sitting on their desks. As they marched like obedient soldiers to the front of the room, they knew this was it. The last strike. The black card.

It was bad enough when they'd been forced to spend lunch break writing the recess rules over and over until their hands cramped to make sure they remembered not to break them again. What would happen now?

A short time later Dieter and Stephen left the principal's office, their shoulders slumped and their expressions dejected. The punishment was harsher than they'd ever imagined. A note would be put in their files for the rest of their elementary and junior high school years. It would read: "Stephen Colletti and Dieter Schmitz are never allowed to be put in the same classroom again."

# LAUREN ANd STEPHEN

## To Dye For

"Just look at yourself, *Stephanie*," Stephen's older brother teased. "You're all *brown*. You look like a piece of poo."

Stephen took a good, long look at himself in the mirror. John was right. Everything about him *was* brown. Brown eyes. Brown hair. Brown skin from the countless hours he spent on the beach. The only thing he lacked to complete the effect was a brown shirt and pants. This was not good. He was in junior high. Looking like poo was not an option.

Stephen needed help. Naturally, he turned to his pal Lauren. True, she had dumped him heartlessly after a week of dating a few years earlier, but he'd long since gotten over that and they were now the best of friends.

"We have to do something about the way I look," he told her.

After vetoing a few radical ideas, the two settled on changing the color of Stephen's hair. Platinum blond? Red? "No way." Stephen shook his head. He could guess what John would say if he walked through the door with bright orange hair. They settled on black instead.

Standing in the hair care aisle of a local drugstore, they

debated what brand to buy. Who would have thought there'd be so many shades of black to choose from? Lauren picked out one for middle-aged men who needed to cover gray hair.

"This should work," she said.

Stephen hesitated. "Are you sure?"

"Sure," she told him confidently, heading for the cash register. "Why not?"

Back at her house a few hours later, Lauren rinsed the color off Stephen's hair as he leaned over the sink.

"It's gonna look great," she assured him. Actually, she had no idea what it would look like. It was impossible to tell with his hair still soaking wet.

Stephen dried his hair and the two of them peered anxiously into the bathroom mirror, eyes fixed on the top of Stephen's head.

"Hey," he said. "It's not so bad."

"Told you so," said Lauren.


"Was that your friend Stephen I saw leaving the house a little while ago?" Lauren's father asked her later that day.

Lauren nodded.

"I almost didn't recognize him," her dad said.

"Well, it's been a while since you guys have seen each other," Lauren responded casually.

"Yes, but something about him looked different," her dad continued.

"Um, I think he might be getting a little taller," said Lauren, trying to hide a smile.

"Hmm," her dad responded absently. "That must've been it."

# KRISTIN

## The Diary Disaster

"Zach is sooooooo cute. Oh my God, I *love* him!"

Kristin finished writing and snapped the cover of her diary shut. She couldn't put the little book away in its usual hiding place because she was on vacation, so instead she slipped it into a drawer in the bedside table. It would be safe there. Wouldn't it? Nobody ever put stuff in those hotel room drawers. Nobody would think to check for it there. Besides, who wants to read a seventh grade girl's diary anyway?

Kristin had brought her diary along on the trip to Hawaii with her dad and her brother thinking she would want to write down all her impressions of the exotic, tropical scenery and the fun stuff that happened while it was fresh in her mind.

She'd been so excited for the trip to start. Her parents had divorced four years earlier, and since then she hadn't gotten to see her dad nearly as often as she would have liked. Being away from him was tough, especially for a daddy's girl like her. And since her brother Mike had gone to Laguna Beach to live with Dad two years ago, when Mom remarried and took Kristin to Chicago to live with her new stepfamily, Kristin even missed him, too. A va-

cation with Dad and Mike was going to be great, and she wanted to write as much of it down in her diary as she could to make sure she didn't forget any of the highlights.

But since her arrival in Hawaii, Kristin had hardly bothered to write a word about the beach or the beautiful sunsets. Instead, she had written pages and pages about Zach, Mike's friend from Laguna who had decided to tag along at the last minute.

To Mike, Zach was just your average ninth grade guy, someone fun to hang out with. But to Kristin, who never saw suntanned Southern California surfers back in the Midwest, Zach was seriously hot. She could hardly take her eyes off him on the beach. So far, she thought she had managed to play it cool. Zach had no idea she liked him.

She changed into her bathing suit, grabbed a towel, and walked out to the beach to lie in the sun and, hopefully, catch sight of her crush. If she kept her sunglasses on he would have no idea she was sneaking admiring glances at him.

There was no sign of Mike or Zach, but Kristin spent an enjoyable afternoon flipping through magazines, watching surfers ride the waves in the distance and little kids splash along the shoreline, and taking a dip in the pool whenever she got too hot. At last, she headed back to her room to shower, change, and meet everyone for dinner.

It would feel good to get all the gritty sand and suntan lotion off her skin, she thought, as she fumbled for her room key. She heard snickering somewhere nearby. It must have been coming from another room.

Finally, she found her key and pushed the door open.

There, sitting on her bed, were Zach and Mike, poring over her diary.

"What are you doing? That's mine!!" Kristin cried, making a lunge for the diary.

Mike snatched it out of her reach easily.

"Oooo, Zach is sooooooo cute!" he sang in a falsetto voice. "He's soooooo dreamy!"

The two of them almost fell off the bed laughing.

Kristin was so mortified she hardly said a word for the rest of the vacation. Her dad couldn't figure out what was wrong. When he asked Mike and Zach if Kristin was feeling okay, they just shrugged and then smirked at each other knowingly when he wasn't looking.

The first thing Kristin did when she got home was to buy a new diary with a lock and key.

A few years later, shortly after Kristin moved to Laguna Beach to live with her dad, she was sitting at home one night when the phone rang.

"Hello?"

"Hey, Kristin," said the voice on the other end. "It's Zach. Remember me?"

How could she forget?

"Want to come to a party with me?"

Kristin said okay, and soon the two of them started hanging out together regularly. They dated for five months before Kristin finally sat him down one night and broke the news that she was ready to move on. She was new to Laguna. She didn't need a serious boyfriend. She needed to make some girlfriends her own age to hang out with. She needed to have fun. Besides, although she didn't say it to Zach's face, hot surfer guys were plentiful around Laguna Beach.

Zach reluctantly agreed to break up. "We'll still be friends, right?" Kristin agreed.

That night, Kristin went home. She changed for bed, brushed her teeth, turned out the light, and fell asleep. She didn't write a single word about what had happened in a diary. In fact, she hadn't owned one since seventh grade.

# Alex M. and Taylor

## He's Mine! The Battle Over Evan

Every girl in fifth grade wanted to trade houses with Alex M. Not because her house was bigger or fancier or closer to the beach than theirs, but because it was next door to the house that Evan, the cute new guy at school, had just moved into with his family.

"Where's he from?" Taylor asked Alex one day at lunch, gazing longingly at Evan across the cafeteria.

"Oregon," Alex told her friend knowledgeably. She already had more inside info about Evan than any other girl did, since she had recently started walking to school with him in the mornings.

"I'm jealous," said Taylor. "He's really cute."

"Yeah, he is," agreed Alex, admiring the earring she could see peeking out from under Evan's blond hair. None of the boys they knew from Laguna Beach were cool enough to wear an earring.

During their morning walks Alex never told Evan that practically every girl at their school was dying to go out with him. She did let him know that *she* thought he was cute, though, and after a few weeks of friendly conversations, he officially became her new boyfriend. Hearts broke all over Top of the World Elementary School.

But not Alex's. Things were going along perfectly for her until one day she went to meet Evan for lunch as usual and spotted him sitting with Taylor.

"What's going on?" she asked, walking up to him.

"I like *her* now," he said.

Speechless, Alex stared from one of them to the other and back, waiting for an explanation. Taylor, pink-cheeked and embarrassed, glanced away, refusing to meet Alex's gaze. For some reason, that made Alex more furious than anything else about the situation. She could deal with Evan's betrayal. She had only known him a few months. And they were only in fifth grade. But she and Taylor had been friends since preschool. She still remembered the days when  Taylor used to suck her thumb. How could an old and trusted friend steal your boyfriend from right under your nose?

This meant war.

Alex and Taylor hadn't gotten into a serious fight since second grade. That one, too, was about a boy. It escalated into a screaming match that landed both of them in the principal's office and left the boy in question—a kid named Michael—blushing furiously at his desk while his classmates teased him about the girlfight he had caused.

This time, instead of yelling at each other in the middle of class, Alex and Taylor launched a cold war of stare-downs, scribbled notes, and hostile whispers. Alex would stand at the center of a cluster of her friends at the top of the hill outside school, glaring down at Taylor and her friends gathered next to the handball courts. She would put her head close to one of her friend's ears for a confidential conference, like a godfather in the mafia. The friend would listen, nod, and then without a word, march dutifully out to no man's land between the two enemy camps to meet one of Taylor's messengers.

"Alex wants to know why Taylor stole her boyfriend!"

"Taylor says to tell Alex it's Evan's decision who he wants to be with!"

"Oh yeah?!"

"Yeah!"

Even their friends were about to come to blows over Evan. So Alex and Taylor finally agreed to call an uneasy truce. Still, Alex couldn't resist the urge to run up to Taylor that spring in the hallway, catching her unaware, and hissing, "Evan doesn't like you anymore. He told me to tell you that."

When she saw the shocked, wounded look on Taylor's face, she gave her an evil grin. "April Fool's!"

But fifth grade boys can be fickle, and by the end of the

year, Evan the heartthrob was with Alex again. In fact, things were getting serious enough that one afternoon he led her into a hidden cave and pulled her close.

He's going to kiss me! Alex thought breathlessly. Wouldn't Taylor be jealous? She closed her eyes and waited.

Yuuuuck! It wasn't what she'd expected at all. This was kissing? Why did people like it so much? She pulled away from him and made an excuse about having to get home. Then she went off to find her friend and tell her the battle was over. As far as she was concerned, if Taylor wanted Evan, she could have him.

# Alex M. and Taylor

### Move Over, Mean Girls

There was no doubt that the eighth grade girl staring them down in the hallway loathed Taylor and Alex M. She either whispered loudly to her friends about them or shouted insults in their direction whenever they walked past. Taylor and Alex, lowly sixth graders still new to junior high, would wilt under the girl's scathing glances and the disdainful sneers of her friends.

Week after week, the girl came up with new ways to harass them. Alex and Taylor weren't sure if she was enough of a bully to risk getting suspended by actually trying to beat them up, but they didn't want to tempt her. Out of self-protection, they changed their routes to class, walking out of their way and arriving just as the bell rang or later in order to avoid the mean girl in the hall.

"You know, if she spends that much time and energy hating younger girls, she's probably not that cool herself," Alex told Taylor as they made their way along their circuitous, time-consuming new route to class. "We should stop letting her intimidate us."

Taylor nodded in agreement. "Those are cool sunglasses," she added. "Are they new?"

"Thanks!" Alex said, smiling at the compliment and adjusting her red Arnette sunglasses. "I just got them."

"You!" a shrill voice broke into their conversation. "Take those sunglasses off!"

Alex and Taylor looked up, startled. There right in front of them, blocking their way to class, stood the eighth grade bully. She had planted herself directly in their path, hands on her hips, her lower lip jutted out angrily. Perched on her nose were the exact same red Arnette sunglasses that Alex was wearing. She looked livid at the idea that she and her sixth grade nemesis were making the same fashion statement. Her cheeks were turning as red with rage as her sunglass frames.

"Take them off now," the girl ordered in a low, menacing voice.

Alex just stood there staring at her. Taylor held her breath.

"I said take them off!"

"No," Alex said suddenly. "You can't tell me what to do. I'm going to wear these to school if I want."

Then she pushed past the girl, clipping her with her shoulder and leaving her standing there dumbfounded, staring after her.

It was the last time either Alex or Taylor ever spoke to the girl. In fact, they saw remarkably little of her in the hallway for the rest of the year.

When seventh grade started, Taylor and Alex were happy to hand over their spots as low women on the totem pole to the incoming sixth graders. It would be nice to have a little seniority, thought Taylor, though she knew she would never make life as miserable for anyone as the older girls had made it for Alex and her.

Then about halfway through the year, she and Alex had a falling out. Neither one of them remembered exactly how the feud started, but before long they weren't speaking to each other.

Alex was the unofficial leader of their clique and, whether it was out of respect or fear, the rest of their friends followed her lead. If Alex wasn't speaking to Taylor, neither were they. Taylor didn't realize how bad things had gotten until she walked up to say "hi" to her former friends one morning and overheard them talking about her. She was devastated. It was all she could do to run to the girls' bathroom before she burst into tears.

Taylor steered clear of them for the next few months, but she hated being alone. She missed her friends. She had no one to laugh with, no one to eat lunch with, and no one to slip notes to when the teacher wasn't looking.

She wondered how Alex could be so mean when she knew how hard and hurtful it was to be on the receiving end. Didn't she remember their first year of junior high when girls had been mean to them? How could she do the same thing to her own friend?

Finally, Taylor had had enough. She decided she would have to go to Alex and apologize for whatever it was she had done.

She spotted Alex alone in the hall one day and walked timidly up to her. "Alex," she asked, "why are you mad at me?"

Alex gave her a disdainful look.

"Whatever it is I did, I'm sorry," said Taylor, tears welling up in her eyes. "You know I don't like to fight."

"All right," Alex said impatiently. "We can be friends again. But you've gotta stop crying and stand up for yourself. Haven't you learned that by now? When are you going to stop letting mean girls intimidate you?"

# Alex M.
## The Number One Fan

"Dear Madonna . . ."

Alex chewed on the end of her pen, debating what to write next. She wanted the letter to be just right. This wasn't the first one she had written to Madonna, but it was the first time she had invited the star to come to Laguna and hang out at the beach with her.

Six-year-old Alex was the world's biggest Madonna fanatic. She belonged to Madonna's fan club, she owned every album Madonna had ever made, and she knew the words to every song Madonna had ever sung. She had created a celebrity collage on the wall above her bed with pictures of Freddie Prinze Jr., Mariah Carey, and all the other stars she liked, but nobody got more wall space than Madonna.

Alex's all-time favorite after-school activity was to dress up like Madonna and dance and sing along to her hits, often with her friends as backup singers. She hoped one day she might be a singer and dancer just like Madonna. Alex came from a musical family, so why couldn't it happen? Her uncle was in a band, and her dad played guitar and sang her to sleep to Bob Marley tunes every night. Alex herself was already involved in musical theater. She was a member of Laguna Tots, a kids' performing troupe that sang parodies of Broadway show tunes. Earlier in the year she had been chosen to play the lead role of Alice in a school production of *Alice in Wonderland* and memorized not just her own lines but everybody else's, too, so that whenever other kids got stuck she could run up and give them their lines.

At last Alex finished her letter. She reread it to make sure it was perfect, then sealed it and walked with her mom to the mailbox to send it to Madonna. She knew it might take a few weeks for Madonna to get the letter and then to make plans for her trip to Laguna Beach, so she tried to be patient.

While she waited for Madonna's response, Alex practiced her singing and dancing (she wanted to be able to impress her favorite star when she finally met her) and imagined how cool it would be to hang out at the beach with someone so famous. She bet Madonna could really use a day of relaxing in the sun and splashing in the waves. Laguna Beach was perfect for that. Alex knew she'd like it.

Every day after school, she hurried home to check the mailbox and tried not to be disappointed when another afternoon went by without an answer from Madonna. After waiting anxiously for two weeks she began to lose hope.

"Shouldn't Madonna have gotten my letter by now?" she asked her mom.

Finally Alex began to suspect that Madonna might never come to Laguna Beach. She might never even write back. When reality sank in, Alex cried every day for a week. She was too depressed to dance or sing, too depressed even to listen to her Madonna CDs.

Then one day, as she shuffled into the house hanging her head, Alex's mom waved an envelope at her. "You got a letter!"

Alex ripped it open eagerly. Inside was a note from Madonna's publicist thanking Alex for the invitation and telling her that while Madonna would love to come visit her and see Laguna Beach, she was a little too busy with her upcoming tour to take a vacation right now. Attached to the letter was an auto-graphed picture from Madonna herself!

It wasn't as good as a visit, but it was the next best thing. Alex hurried to her room and carefully placed her brand-new personally signed picture of Madonna at the top of her collage. Then she cranked up the Madonna tunes and started dancing. Maybe Madonna wouldn't be so busy after her tour. Maybe then she would have time to take Alex up on her offer. Alex wanted to be ready if she did.

She was still practicing, dancing and singing, when her mom knocked on her door several hours later.

"Alex," she said. "Dinner's ready."

"Okay, Mom," Alex said, barely pausing from her dance routine. "I'll be there in a minute." She'd take a break right after the next song. Or maybe the one after that.

# Taylor

*The Truth*

Taylor awoke in the wee hours of Christmas morning. She wasn't sure exactly what time it was, but she knew it must be very early because the house was silent and the first gray rays of daylight were just beginning to brighten the yard outside her window.

Brimming with excitement, she climbed out of bed, tiptoed out of her room, and crept downstairs as quietly as she could. What would Santa bring this year? She couldn't wait to find out.

She bounded into the living room, past the Christmas tree and over to the mantel where her stocking was hanging. She reached up and tugged on it eagerly. Instead of falling down into her lap bulky and heavy with gifts, it slipped lightly into her hands. She peered inside. Empty.

Taylor checked her sister's stocking. It was empty, too. So were her parents' stockings. Next, she bent down and checked underneath the tree. There were no presents anywhere. Had Santa forgotten them? She quickly replayed the last twelve months in her mind. Had she really done anything so bad that Santa would decide to skip her this year?

Frantic, she raced upstairs and burst into her parents' room. "Mommy!" she sobbed. "Mommy!"

Her mom, still bleary-eyed with sleep, sat up in alarm. "What's the matter, Taylor?" she asked, looking worried. "What happened?"

"It's Santa! He didn't come!"

"Oh no," her mom moaned, looking even more alarmed. "We forgot to put out the presents!"

"What?!" Taylor's mouth fell open.

Her mom tried to backpedal, but it was too late. The secret was out.

Christmas would never be the same again, thought Taylor as she surveyed the mounds of torn wrapping paper and newly opened gifts. Still, she reminded herself, knowing the truth was better than worrying that Santa had decided to pass you by all together if you happened to be the first one to wake up on Christmas morning.

# Taylor

## Sinking

With the sky a brilliant shade of blue and the wind picking up nicely, Taylor thought it looked like a perfect day for sailing as her dad guided their forty-foot boat out of the harbor and set a course for Catalina Island. At ten years old, she was already an old hand on deck, deftly helping with the sails and the rudder as her dad instructed.

Taylor had been sailing for as long as she could remember—almost as long as she had been walking. She was always inviting her friends to come with her, but none of them shared her passion for the sport. She was the only one who seemed to feel more comfortable on a boat than she did on land.

The gorgeous weather and brisk winds kept up, and the family spent an enjoyable day sailing around Catalina. They had just turned the boat around and were heading back toward the mainland in the late afternoon when they heard a frightening *crack*. To their horror, they realized that the shaft, which connects to the rudder at the bottom of the boat, had broken off. In its place was an enormous hole that was fast filling up with water. If they didn't act quickly, the boat would sink.

Keeping his voice calm and steady to make sure no one panicked, Taylor's dad instructed her sixteen-year-old cousin Greg to take a white shirt up to the bow and try to flag down a passing powerboat for help. In the meantime, he did his best to plug the gaping hole in the hull before radioing the Coast Guard of their location more than twenty miles offshore.

A tense hour passed as family members alternately checked to make sure the leak wasn't getting worse, squinted hopefully into the horizon in search of the Coast Guard, and waved desperately at passing pleasure boats to attract their attention. At last, a stranger in a powerboat recognized their distress signal, pulled up alongside their damaged boat, and offered to tow them in.

Taylor still loved sailing (she went on to compete in sailing in the Junior Olympics three times), but she had never been so grateful to see the California coastline coming into view. She clambered eagerly off the deck and onto the pier. She would be back on the water in no time, but for that night at least she understood precisely why her friends felt more comfortable on dry land than they did on a boat.

# Alex M.

## *The Dream Role*

Alex's grandfather introduced her to musicals when she was just a toddler. By age thirteen, she adored them as much as he did. On movie nights, when she and her eight cousins would pile into his living room and every kid got a turn to pick a movie, Alex always went for a musical. Usually she chose *The Sound of Music,* which was not only her favorite but her grandfather's, too. She loved the character Leisl, the pretty teenage daughter who sang "Sixteen Going on Seventeen."

Naturally, when Alex learned that the local musical theater workshop where she often performed was doing a summer production of *The Sound of Music* she was first in line to audition. She already knew every word to every song and almost every line of dialogue by heart. She would have gladly accepted any role, but when the director told her she had landed the part of Leisl, it was all she could do to restrain herself from hugging him.

Rehearsals flew by and in no time the cast was getting into

costume, putting on their makeup, and taking their places as the curtain opened on the first night of the show. It didn't matter that it was only a local production performed for a small audience in a small theater. To Alex, playing Leisl was the role of a lifetime.

Perhaps the best moment of all came not onstage, but after the cast took their bows and hurried backstage to their dressing rooms. That was when Alex caught sight of her beaming grandfather rushing up to congratulate her, a big bouquet of flowers in his hands.

"Alex," he said. "That was even better than the original!"

# TALAN

## The First Date

Talan had lots of girl *friends,* but there was something special about Britney, who lived next door. She was cute. She was fun. She was funny. He loved hanging out with her, but he was ten now. Old enough for more than just hanging out. There was no doubt in Talan's mind: He wanted to ask Britney out on a date.

"I'd like to take Britney to dinner," he told his mom one day. "Do you mind if I do that?"

"Well, you'll need to ask her mom first."

Talan worked up his nerve and did what his mom suggested. Britney's mom agreed. Then she talked to Talan's mother, and the two of them decided they would tag along just in case, but would keep their distance and not interfere. "You won't even know we're there," his mom promised.

Since this was going to be a special night, Talan needed something special to wear. He cruised through several stores and spent a long time debating over what to buy. He finally settled on a new V-neck sweater.

Next, he visited a local flower shop. What was Britney's favorite color? Red? Pink? Yellow? Should he choose a bunch of different ones? He selected a bouquet he hoped she'd like and headed for home. Time was running out.

A short time later, showered and dressed, Talan combed his hair and stepped back to inspect his image in the mirror. Satisfied, he scooped up the flowers and went next door to Britney's house.

Even Britney's mom was struck by the transformation when Talan knocked on the door. He was the same kid who was always outside playing soccer, tossing a football around, or toting his surfboard to the beach and back, but he was so polite. He'd brought flowers and everything.

The four of them—Britney, Talan, and the two moms—drove to an Italian restaurant and got out of the car. Talan knew a guy could get embarrassed by a situation like this if he thought about it, but he wasn't going to let that ruin his first date.

"Table for two," he told the hostess. He could tell what she was thinking: Isn't that sweet? Aren't they adorable? But he ignored it and sat down across from Britney. Meanwhile, their moms seated themselves at another table a safe distance away.

Having grandparents from Italy, Talan was an old pro when it came to Italian food. He explained some of the unfamiliar sounding dishes listed on the menu to his date, then ordered for her. When they finished dinner, he paid the bill with money his mom had given him ahead of time.

Afterward, they strolled next door and got ice cream. Since Talan and Britney were good friends from the neighborhood, they chatted easily and laughed together as always. As far as first dates went, this one was about as comfortable and nonawkward as it gets.

Later that evening, when they finally got a moment away

from their well-meaning moms, Talan would put the finishing touch on the night by closing his eyes and getting his first kiss.

Within a few months, he'd consider himself an old pro in the kissing department, offering to share his expertise with the girls he knew. "Hey," he'd say. "Let me teach you how to kiss." The kisses might have meant a little less as time went on, but Talan never stopped being a hopeless romantic. He was always the first one to admit it.

# Talan

## Big Brother to the Rescue . . . Almost

Lorenzo was missing. Talan's mom was trying not to show how worried she was, but eight-year-old Talan could see it written all over her face. His little brother had been at the park across the street just a few minutes ago. The housekeeper kept apologizing all over the place. She'd been sure he was right behind her. Then she turned around and he was nowhere in sight.

Talan didn't wait to hear more. He jumped on his bike and headed off in search of Lorenzo. How far could a five-year-old kid have wandered by now? Which way could he have gone? Toward the beach? Away from it?

Lorenzo had to be somewhere in their neighborhood of Emerald Bay, Talan figured. If he searched long enough, he was bound to find him. But the hills were steep, and it was hard, sweaty work pedaling up every one of them trying to watch where you were going *and* keep an eye out for your little brother. Talan kept his eyes open so wide they stung in the wind.

So, *this* was what it felt like to be a parent. He was beginning to have a lot more sympathy for his mom and dad. It must be the worst thing in the world to worry like this all the time.

Finally, he grew so exhausted that he decided to stop back home to see whether anyone else had heard any news of Lorenzo. As he neared his house, he hit the brakes, jumped off the bike, and ran inside.

"Mom!" he called, rounding a corner and stopping short. His mouth fell open.

There, sitting contentedly with his mother, was Lorenzo.

"Where were you?!" Talan exclaimed. He stopped short of adding, "I was worried sick!"

"He was right down the street the whole time," Talan's mom told him.

As it turned out, Lorenzo had simply walked off down the block and—appropriately enough—wandered into the neighborhood lost and found. Just off the beach, the area was filled with a colorful assortment of misplaced boogie boards, forgotten towels, beach chairs waiting to be reclaimed by their owners, and plenty of toys to entertain a five-year-old. When Lorenzo had gotten bored of playing, he'd walked out again. A neighbor had spotted him and brought him home, none the worse for wear.

Talan wasn't sure whether to punch Lorenzo for scaring him so badly or hug him because he was so glad to see him. Since their parents' divorce, Talan had felt even more protective of his brother. They loved both of their parents and spent lots of time with each of them, but divorce was hard on a kid any way you sliced it. He decided to go for the hug.

"Get off me!" said Lorenzo, squirming away from his older brother.

Talan's mom smiled as she watched. Lorenzo was a lucky kid to have a big brother like Talan.

# TALAN
## The Four Most Important Seconds
## of Seventh Grade

So it all came down to this. Four seconds on the clock. Talan had loved football for as long as he could remember. Loved watching it. Loved playing it. He even loved movies about football. And he loved playing quarterback.

But tonight the odds were stacked against them. Long Beach was a formidable opponent. The linemen looked huge enough from Talan's twelve-year-old perspective to be NFL players. He could tell by their smirking, disdainful glances that most of the team was scoffing at the little surfer dudes from Laguna. What did these guys do? Get lost on their way to the beach and end up on the gridiron? Long Beach *never* lost to Laguna Beach. Ever.

To add to tonight's pressure cooker, Talan's dad was his coach. And he sure didn't believe in taking it easier on his own kid when it came to football. One of his favorite ways to assure the rest of the team that he wasn't playing favorites was to make his own son run extra laps.

But deep down, Talan knew his dad believed in him fiercely. He had chosen his son's unusual name in part because it reminded him of the talons of an eagle, soaring above it all. Tonight Talan thought it might be hard to live up to that.

The fourth quarter was winding down and, miraculously, Talan and his teammates had held their opponents at zero. Talan hadn't lost his focus despite a wicked cut to the shin that was bleeding freely through his sock and leaving a red stain down to his cleat.

And now it was do or die. Just four seconds were left in the game. Laguna Beach was at the three-yard line. Maddeningly close.

"All you've gotta do is run those three yards and drop the ball in, Talan," his dad told him.

"Dad, these guys have never lost to us," Talan said. "They're not just gonna move aside so I can run the ball in."

His dad shrugged. "It's up to you," he said, and stepped away.

All of Talan's twelve years seemed to be leading up to this moment, this play.

The ball slipped into Talan's hands. He faked a handoff, dodged out of reach of the linemen charging toward him, and dived for the goal line as the final whistle blew.

That was it. Game over.

Final score? 6-0 Laguna Beach. The little surfer dudes had pulled it off.

Talan caught a glimpse of beaming faces before his teammates piled on top of him in a shouting, celebrating heap. He hardly remembered leaving the field. He hardly remembered the rest of the night.

Years later he would play quarterback for Laguna Beach High School in the same stadium, the stands filled with fans, cheerleaders lining the sidelines. But no high school game ever surpassed the sheer adrenaline of those four seconds against Long Beach as a twelve-year-old Pop Warner player.

# TALAN
## Lucky 13 (From Stoked to Soaked)

For as long as he could remember Talan had been a Steelers fan. Having a dad who was a Pittsburgh native, a football fanatic, and a youth football coach pretty much meant that in Talan's family you were *born* a Steelers fan. It didn't matter that you lived in Southern California, two thousand miles away from Heinz Field.

Almost every inch of wall space in Talan's room was covered with autographed pictures of Steelers players. What little room was left went to Italian soccer posters. (Talan's grandfather had once played on Italy's National Soccer Team, and Talan had grown to love the sport, listening to his grandfather's stories of his glory days on the field. He could never decide which he liked better—his grandfather's soccer stories or his tales of fighting in the Italian mountains in World War II.)

So, when Talan's mom surprised him with tickets to a Steelers-49ers game for his thirteenth birthday, he was stoked. Going to San Francisco was a treat in itself. Getting to see his favorite team play was even better. Plus, thirteen was a landmark birthday—the start of your life as a teenager.

Since this was a special treat for Talan, his brother Lorenzo stayed home. It was just Talan and his mom who headed to San Francisco that weekend. The trip turned out to be fun, and so far the game was even better than he'd hoped. The Steelers had the ball when Talan felt a drop of water hit his head. Then another. And another.

"I think it's starting to rain."

Within seconds, the skies opened up. The rain pouring down was so heavy they could barely see. Talan and his mom had no choice but to make a dash for the gates with the rest of the soaking wet crowd.

Outside the stadium, drenched and shivering, they scanned the mammoth parking lot hopefully for arriving cabs. But since no one had expected the game to end at this hour, there were none to be found. When a city bus pulled up at the curb they boarded it in desperation. They had no idea where it was going, but anything had to be better than standing in the downpour any longer.

They peered out the rain-streaked windows, but nothing in the gray cityscape the bus passed looked familiar. Finally, after asking directions and transferring buses again, the two eventually found themselves at Fisherman's Wharf around dinnertime.

The rain had stopped at last, so they walked along the pier, glancing in restaurant windows, checking out the menus posted outside, and debating which seafood place looked most tempting. They settled on one with a dark interior and a cozy fireplace in the center of the dining room.

The waitstaff obligingly seated them at a table next to the fire. Talan followed his mom's lead, pulling off his wet gloves and setting them on the hearth's edge to dry next to the flames.

By the time dinner arrived, Talan and his mom were laughing about the unexpected turn of events. Somehow the downpour seemed much funnier once you were out of it. And at least one thing was certain: The day had been a memorable one.

As Talan sat in the glow of the crackling fire, eating sticky ginger crab and feeling his soggy clothes begin to dry and his skin to warm up under them, he decided that all in all, this wasn't such a bad way to start life as a teenager.

# JESSICA

*Fitting In*

Jessica slammed the door of her room and flopped down on her princess bed, staring hard at the pink walls covered in posters of Justin Timberlake as she fought the urge to cry. It just wasn't fair. *Life* wasn't fair.

It was bad enough finding out that her parents were getting divorced. But now they had told her she was going to have to leave Phoenix and move all the way to California.

Laguna Beach was fine for vacations (Jessica's grandparents had a summer house there, and she and her younger sister Diana had been visiting for years), but all of Jessica's friends, her school, and everything else she knew was in Phoenix. She would have to start all over. Make new friends. Find her way around a new school. And do it all right in the middle of sixth

grade. To a twelve-year-old girl it was almost the worst fate imaginable.

Everything about Laguna Beach was a culture shock for Jessica when she arrived. While the junior high schools in Phoenix were equipped with metal detectors at the doors and had cops on standby around the building, Laguna was a small, sleepy town where no one worried about kids showing up for class packing weapons. Jessica's mom was delighted about how much safer the new location would be for her daughters.

But Jessica noticed a lot of other differences, too. The girls here looked and dressed nothing like Jessica and her friends in Phoenix did. They all wore Roxy clothes and had superstraight, sun-streaked hair from the hours they spent on the beach. Jessica, by contrast, arrived sporting the latest in preteen Phoenix fashions: permed hair and blue acrylic nails with white tips. She didn't even look like an inlander. She looked like a tourist.

Worse, every girl she saw seemed to be rail thin. Jessica was curvy, with a bustline that already drew enough whistles from passing guys to make her blush. Even her mom teased her about her figure.

And everybody was rich. Even the kids who claimed to be middle-class were pretty sheltered in her opinion. She was used to seeing homeless people in downtown Phoenix. Nobody would ever let someone sleep in a cardboard box on the streets of Laguna Beach.

Just to make life more complicated, the cutoff age for starting school in Laguna was different from the one in Phoenix. That meant the administration at Jessica's new school decided to have her skip the rest of sixth grade and go straight into seventh instead. Overnight, she went from being the oldest kid in class to being the youngest.

The one upside was how friendly her new classmates seemed. Jessica had feared they would be hopelessly cliquey since most of them had grown up together and known each other all their lives, but on her very first day at school, girls invited her to sit with them at lunch. Before long, she had a whole new group of friends.

She brought one of them along for advice when she went shopping for school clothes. Afterward, she threw out her old wardrobe to make room for a new one more in keeping with the casual Laguna sense of style. Next, she ditched the elaborately manicured nails and counted the days until her perm grew out.

By the time the school year ended, it seemed to Jessica as if she had been living in Laguna Beach all her life. She finally felt at home.

Still, summer vacation meant a trip back to Phoenix to see all her old friends. She couldn't wait to fill them in on everything that had happened since she left. She was shocked when they teased her about looking like a rich snob with her straight hair and beach bum clothes. "I haven't changed," she told them. "I'm exactly the same person."

But she could tell by their skeptical looks they didn't believe her. In a way she couldn't blame them. She had felt the same way herself not long ago. Laguna Beach was just one of those places you couldn't truly understand unless you lived there.

# Alex H., Cedric, and Jessica
## Getting the Laguna Look

When Alex H.'s family moved from Lake Tahoe to Laguna Beach during the summer before fourth grade, nine-year-old Alex was more than happy to trade snow for sun and surf. Since she had already lived in San Diego, Utah, *and* Nevada, she wasn't worried about adjusting to a new place. She figured she could fit in easily just about anywhere.

She soon had a new friend named Morgan S. and a new boyfriend named Cedric. Like Alex and Morgan, Cedric lived in the gated community of Three Arch Bay and was getting ready to start fourth grade.

Everything was going well when Cedric sat Alex down for a talk one afternoon shortly before the first day of school.

"Look," he said. "I really like you, but . . ."

Uh-oh, thought Alex. Here it comes. He's dumping me.

Cedric glanced away as if trying to find a delicate way to phrase what he had to say next. "You have *got* to do something about your clothes."

"What's wrong with my clothes?!" exclaimed Alex, glancing down self-consciously at her pink overall shorts and T-shirt.

"Alex," he said confidentially. "Let me give you some advice. Nobody wears those. You can't go to school dressed like that. Everyone will think you're a dork. Here's what you need."

He rattled off a lengthy shopping list, including board shorts, low-rise jeans, and Rocket Dog sandals. Alex hurried off to tell her mom they needed to go school shopping ASAP.

Fourth grade started and Alex's love affair with Cedric went the way of most nine-year-olds' romances: It was over in a week or two. By the next year, Alex was infatuated with Sam instead. She spent most of fifth grade recess chasing him around the school fields in her Rocket Dog sandals with the rest of the girls, hoping to pin him down and kiss him.

By sixth grade, when Alex and the other kids from El Morro Elementary moved on to junior high and met the incoming students from Top of the World Elementary, hardly anybody except Alex herself remembered that she had once been a newcomer, struggling to fit into life in the Bubble. When a new girl arrived halfway through seventh grade, Alex's heart went out to her. After all, she had been in that girl's shoes not so many years ago.

Well, not exactly *those* shoes. Jessica seemed really sweet, but her clothes? Alex couldn't let her walk around that way. Everyone would think she was a dork. So one day she sat her down for a talk.

"Jessica," she said confidentially. "Let me give you some advice . . ."

# DIETER

*George Washington and the*
*Green-Eyed Monster*

"There's no reason to be nervous, dear," the teacher said. "Now try it again."

This was about the fifth time Dieter had forgotten one of his lines. His teacher, convinced that he was suffering from a severe case of stage fright, kept trying to calm him down.

But Dieter didn't need that kind of reassurance. He was stoked to be cast in the lead role of George Washington in his fifth grade class play. He and Stephen had already played fairies (with costumes and makeup and everything) in a short movie directed by one of Dieter's older brothers. Dieter loved acting. He knew he wouldn't freeze up when he walked onstage wearing a powdered wig in front of his entire elementary school.

No, his nerves were definitely not the problem. His girlfriend, Leigh, was the problem.

Leigh, too, was in the play. She only had a small part, but it required her to stand next to another boy in their class the whole time she was onstage.

Dieter didn't trust the boy at all. He saw the way the kid kept grinning at Leigh and trying to catch her attention whenever he thought Dieter wasn't looking. Whenever their scene ended and they walked offstage together, Dieter's concentration went right offstage with them. His suspicions about what might be going on behind the curtain while he was stuck rehearsing some speech about Valley Forge almost drove him crazy. He cast a suspicious glance at the boy. Definitely sketchy, he thought.

"Try again, dear," the teacher prompted. Dieter cleared his throat and repeated his line.

"I'm *not* flirting with him!" Leigh protested after the rehearsal, but Dieter felt jealous all the same. He couldn't stand the idea of some random guy—some random guy with a bit part, no less—hitting on his girlfriend behind his back.

When the day of the performance finally arrived, Dieter did his best to focus on the play. Instead of fighting back his emotions, he tried to channel them into his performance. At last the curtains closed and the cast took their bows, Dieter at the center.

When the applause died away, the teacher rushed up to congratulate her students. "Very good!" she said, beaming at Dieter.

She was amazed at how her star's stage fright seemed to melt away in front of an audience. She saw him throw one or two of those weird glances backstage that always made him look like he was waiting to be prompted on a line, but not nearly as many as he used to do in rehearsals. Yes, she thought, her reassurance must have worked. Dieter had turned out to be a fine George Washington . . . perhaps a slightly *angrier* George Washington than she was used to seeing, but a fine George all the same.

# DIETER

Dieter gnawed on his bottom lip as he gazed over the prizes lined up on the teacher's desk. His eyes flicked back and forth between the soccer ball and the game tickets. There was some gnarly stuff here, and Dieter got first dibs.

All year long, students in his fifth grade class had earned one point for every A on an assignment. To Dieter's amazement, he had somehow ended up with more As—and more points— than anyone else. Now, with summer vacation just around the bend, the teacher had surprised her students by bringing in a bag of tempting goodies and spreading them out on top of her desk.

Students were lined up to cash in their points, some craning their necks around their classmates to get a better look at the graft, others crossing their fingers and praying nobody else would grab the prize they wanted before their turn came.

Dieter's eyes lingered on the soccer ball. He played soccer all the time. He could get a lot of use out of a new ball. Then again, he loved sports events. And there were two tickets, which meant he'd be able to bring Stephen or Trey or another friend along to the game.

Then he spotted the nail polish kit. It was a big, fancy one with lots of different shades of pink and red and purple. He bet every girl in the class had her eye on it.

Ever since his jealous outbursts during the class play, Dieter had wanted to find a way to apologize to his girlfriend,

Leigh, for suspecting her of flirting with one of their classmates and to show her how much he liked her. What would say "I'm sorry" to a fifth grade girl better than a deluxe nail polish kit?

But the kit would cost Dieter every one of his hard-earned points—points it had taken him an entire school year to accumulate.

A few of the boys behind him in line fidgeted restlessly, impatient to see what prize Dieter would take off the table before they got to it. Probably that sweet soccer ball or those choice tickets. Which would he snag?

Dieter hesitated. He gazed longingly at the soccer ball one last time. Then he made his decision.

He collected his prize and stepped away from the teacher's desk, the boys behind him swarming in to take his place.

Without a word, he handed the nail polish kit to Leigh.

# Trey

### Pillow Talk

Home economics wasn't exactly the high point of the day for your average sixth grade guy. Trey was no exception. This week's assignment: Make a pillow using various fabrics, a sewing machine, and a pattern.

Trey cut the material and set to work. Before he knew it, the class had flown by. He was amazed at how much fun he was having. By far the best part was the end result. Even if it was just a pillow, he was pumped knowing that he had created it. He'd taken it from point A to point B, turned it from a pile of cloth and thread into something real. Trey asked the teacher if he could make another one.

"Sure," she said, surprised. She even gave him extra credit for his second pillow. As far as she knew, he was probably the first boy in the history of home economics classes to actually request an additional sewing project.

# CHRISTINA

## "Who's That Kid?"

Christina's family had been going to the Collettis' house forever. With their moms being best friends since childhood, it was no surprise that Christina had known Stephen and his older sister Lauren practically since they were all in diapers. In fact, she'd spent years hanging out with Lauren, wishing that bratty little brother of hers would just go away and play somewhere else. She couldn't believe it when she finally realized that it was she and Stephen—and not she and Lauren—who were the same age. By the time they got to grade school, Christina had decided Stephen was past the bratty stage and they became great friends, too.

Even though they didn't go to school together, she saw the Collettis all the time. The families took the Schullers' boat on vacation together to Catalina Island every year, and the kids always went to one another's birthday parties. She still laughed every time she remembered Stephen being the only boy at her all-girl, all-pink party at age six. No doubt he was a good friend. After all, the poor guy had shown up in a pink polo shirt in honor of the occasion and been a good sport throughout an afternoon surrounded by giggly girls and decorations that looked like cotton candy.

So, now that Stephen was turning thirteen, naturally Christina showed up for his party, gift in hand. Even though she went to a different school, it wasn't too bad hanging out with Stephen's friends. She'd been going to his parties for so long that she knew them pretty well.

"Hey, Christina," Stephen called, spotting her across the room as she walked in.

"Happy birthday!" she said, going over to greet him.

Soon she felt as at home as always, chatting with Lauren, Dieter, and Stephen's other friends.

When the music started, Christina joined in the dancing with everyone else. She glanced up and spotted a weird-looking

kid she'd never seen before standing on a chair. He seemed to be ignoring everyone else in the room and grooving to his own beat. He had messy blond hair and (*what* was he wearing?) a black leather jacket with sunglasses. Nobody their age wore black leather and sunglasses inside.

"Who is that guy?" she asked the girl next to her.

"Oh, him. That's Trey," the girl said.

Christina fought the urge to ask, Who does he think he is?

"He's been Stephen's friend, like, forever," the girl told her. "He's a little weird with the way he dresses and everything, but he's okay. He's a cool guy."

Christina was skeptical, but she decided to keep an open mind.

# STEPHEN AND TREY
## The First Meeting

Moving from San Juan Capistrano to Laguna Beach was a happy occasion for four-year-old Stephen. First off, he already felt perfectly comfortable in his new house. It had been his grandparents' home before they moved to an island near Vancouver, and Stephen and his older brother and sister had been going to visit them there all their lives. Second, the house was located in Bluebird Canyon, right near the beach, which meant Stephen got to play in the sand and splash in the waves almost every day. Third, he'd soon be old enough to start kindergarten, which was bound to be more exciting than preschool in San Juan Capistrano.

Stephen's mom walked him to the bus stop a couple of times before school started so they could get used to the routine. On one of their walks, they bumped into another mom with a boy about Stephen's age. While the moms introduced themselves and struck up a conversation, Stephen smiled hello to the boy, then glanced around the bus stop, wondering what it would be like to ride a bus to school every day.

"See? You'll have lots of kids from the neighborhood in your kindergarten class," his mom assured him as they walked home. "It'll be fun."

She was right. Kindergarten was fun. A few days after

school started in the fall, a boy came up to him on the playground and tapped his shoulder.

"Hey," he said. "Remember me?"

Stephen looked at the kid. There was definitely something familiar about the blond hair and the friendly smile. All of a sudden he remembered. It was Phil, from his old preschool in San Juan Capistrano.

"Hey, Phil!" he said. "What are you doing here?"

The boy's face fell.

"No," he said. "I'm Trey. We met at the bus stop."

Maybe it wasn't the most promising way to start a friendship, but soon Stephen and Trey were inseparable. They met each other at the bus stop every morning and made sure they got a seat together on the way home every afternoon. On Saturdays and Sundays, they hung out together at the beach or at each other's houses. Within a few weeks it felt as if they'd known each other forever. Stephen found it hard to believe he'd ever mistaken Trey for anyone else.

# TREY
## *Home Sweet School*

If it hadn't been for the idea of leaving his friends, Trey would have been stoked to get out of school. Permanently. He'd overheard his parents talking and he knew they were underwhelmed with the elementary schools in Laguna Beach, so he wasn't surprised when his mom told him she was going to start homeschooling him in first grade.

Stephen promised not to lose touch. And he stayed true to his word, stopping by just about every day after school and dropping in on weekends to pick up Trey on his way to the beach, where they'd hang out all day. In the evenings, they'd often crawl out the window onto Trey's roof and talk some more. It was hard to miss the guy when he was at your house all the time.

Trey had to admit, home school was fun. Before long, he found himself forming opinions about all kinds of things, like the

Civil War and Andrew Jackson's policy toward Native Americans. While his friends were cracking open boring textbooks, he was heading off to the Exploratorium with Mom for their version of science class. He could ask a question whenever he wanted. He didn't even have to raise his hand. And he never had to worry about dress codes or bathroom passes.

Though his school day was shorter than theirs, his coursework was more disciplined than his friends would ever have believed. Combined with the Phillips family's long-standing tradition of lively dinner table discussions about current events and politics every night, Trey knew he was getting a great education. Sometimes he'd forget he wasn't talking with his family and mention current events or historical issues around his friends only to get a blank look or dead silence. But since he played a lot of team sports and spent countless hours boogie boarding, skateboarding, and kicking a soccer ball around with the guys from the neighborhood, he still got plenty of chances to bond with his closest friends. By second grade that list had expanded to include Dieter, who he met through Stephen and who soon became as frequent a guest at the Phillips's house as Stephen.

On nights after soccer matches or baseball games, when he'd finished his homework and was absently sketching out ideas for ways to improve the look of his uniform (why did his teams always have such *boring* jerseys?), he'd often think about how lucky he was. Sure, he sometimes felt a twinge of jealousy when Dieter and Stephen talked about elementary school. They never made him feel bad on purpose, but sometimes it was hard not to feel left out when they were making inside jokes about getting sent to the yellow line again during recess.

"Dude, we *live* on the yellow line," one of them would say and the other would crack up.

"What's the yellow line?" Trey would ask, beginning to suspect he might be missing out on important stuff.

But then either Dieter or Stephen would start griping about how dull math was or how hard that history test last Friday had been, and Trey would casually drop the bomb.

"My mom and I hung out on the couch last Friday and ate nachos while we talked about history. It was really cool."

His friends would stare at him in disbelief, and Trey knew it was their turn to feel a twinge of jealousy.

# CHRISTINA
## What's In a Name?

Aside from getting teased about being a preacher's kid, Christina felt she was pretty much like everyone else in her public school, just another Southern California kid. So it was a shock when she transferred to Rancho Capistrano Christian School in second grade and found out that she was part of what every student there considered a famous family.

Not only was the school located on the campus of the Crystal Cathedral Ministries, which Christina's grandfather had founded, but her father was the top administrator. "You're a Schuller?" her classmates would ask incredulously. "Your dad's, like, the boss of the entire school!"

It hurt Christina's feelings when people avoided or harassed her just because of her last name. Did they think she was a snob? Did they assume she was a tattletale, who would run off and rat on them to her father if they stepped out of line?

She felt so discouraged that she begged her mom to let her go back to public school so she wouldn't have to deal with it. Her mom gave her two pieces of advice that she never forgot. First, she said, "What people think about you is none of your business." Second, she told her, "You can't run away from your problems or you'll never solve them."

The more Christina thought about it, the more sense it made. Kids in her class would think whatever they wanted no matter how hard she tried to change their minds. As long as *she* knew who she was, did their opinion really matter? She might as well stay and tough it out at the new school.

So she did, and things got better over time. As Christina got to know all the kids in her class, she realized that many of them were battling preconceived ideas and prejudices just like she was. Some had gotten into trouble and been kicked out of public school before enrolling in Rancho Capistrano. The other students avoided them just like they had avoided her, so she made a special point to be open-minded and friendly with everyone, and not to judge people without giving them a chance.

Kids might have had some blind spots, but they were nothing compared to adults, as Christina discovered in sixth grade.

That year the principal resigned and started a firestorm among parents. They divided themselves into two groups—those who were happy the principal had left and those who were furious about it. Some who were angry about the change in school staff blamed Christina's dad because of his position in the administration.

Soon parents were arguing angrily and picketing outside the school. Christina's family awoke numerous times to find signs with hostile messages on their mailbox and garage door. It reached a crisis when the family pulled into the school parking lot one morning and found themselves surrounded by picketers. Many of them started pounding on the car windows and shouting. Christina stared out at them, her eyes wide with fear and surprise. What was the matter with these people? They were grown-ups. Couldn't they see that there were frightened children inside the car? Wasn't this supposed to be a school where people followed Christ's teachings about love and peace?

The incident alarmed Christina's parents enough that they sat down at the dinner table that night to discuss whether their children should leave the school. They worried that all the anger toward Christina's father as the most visible administrator and toward the family because of its relation to the school's founder might get misdirected toward Christina and her siblings.

Christina reminded them of what her mom had taught her a few years earlier. First, you can't worry about what other people think. Second, you can't run away from difficult situations. The only way to get through a problem is to face it.

# Morgan S. and Alex H.

## Trick or Treat

One of the best things about having Alex H. as a friend was spending the night at her house in Three Arch Bay. A twelve-year-old girl could never run out of fun things to do there or cute boys to spy on. Since actually hanging out with cute boys was far better than spying on them, Alex and Morgan often walked over to Talan's house to jump on his trampoline or to Sam's to watch skimboard and skateboard videos. Sometimes a group of them would "borrow" the Three Arch golf carts, even though they weren't supposed to, and launch a spirited game of golf cart tag.

Come Halloween, Three Arch was a wonderful place to go trick or treating. Morgan always looked forward to dressing up and going to Alex's to meet all the Three Arch kids. This year was going to be extraspecial because her mom was making a supercool, supercute leopard minidress for her to wear as part of her Pebbles from *The Flintstones* costume.

"So, you're coming over for Halloween, right?" Alex asked Morgan one day.

Morgan nodded enthusiastically. "I can't wait. What costume are you going to wear?"

"It's a surprise," Alex said slyly. "What are *you* wearing?"

"Mine is a surprise, too," Morgan answered. If Alex wasn't telling, neither was she.

On Halloween night, Morgan slipped on her leopard-print dress, pulled her hair into a ponytail, fastened it with a bow in the shape of a giant bone, and hurried off to Alex's house. She couldn't wait to see what everyone else was wearing. She hoped they would all think her Pebbles dress was as cute as she did. Especially the boys.

Morgan knocked impatiently on Alex's front door. "Trick or treat!" she called cheerfully as it swung open.

There stood Alex, wearing a Pebbles outfit almost identical to Morgan's, right down to the leopard-print minidress and the bone-shaped hair bow. They didn't speak to each other the whole night.

# MORGAN S.
## The Celine Dion Standoff

Nobody bothered to ask what Morgan was planning to do in the fifth grade talent show. Since she spent virtually every day after school at Tyne Dance Academy taking lessons in jazz, tap, ballet, lyrical, and hip-hop and was widely acknowledged as one of the best dancers in school, they already knew that her performance would be a dance number. That was hardly news.

What *was* news was how many girls planned to sing this year. They were all being very mysterious about it, too. When curious classmates would ask what song they had chosen, they would only smile coyly and chirp, "You'll see."

The blockbuster movie *Titanic* had just come out and taken the preteen population by storm. Most of the girls in Morgan's elementary school were swooning over Leonardo DiCaprio. It wasn't uncommon to catch students humming the hit theme song "My Heart Will Go On" as they made their way to class. Even boys did it occasionally, when they thought no one would overhear. If Morgan's friends weren't chattering about tryouts for the talent show at lunchtime, they were gushing about how gorgeous Leo was.

Morgan couldn't get the *Titanic* theme song out of her head as she hurried to the school auditorium to audition for the show. When she walked in she was surprised to hear angry voices coming from the stage.

She soon spotted the cause of the commotion. A group of girls was standing in a circle quarreling loudly as the teacher in charge of the show tried in vain to separate them.

"I had it first!" shouted one, planting her hands on her hips defiantly.

"No you didn't!" said another, glaring at her. The two of them looked mad enough to punch each other.

"Calm down everyone," the teacher said. "We'll think of a solution."

"What happened?" Morgan whispered, stepping up to a girl who was watching from the side of the stage. The girl seemed to be fighting the urge to break into hysterical laughter.

"They all want to sing the same song!" she said and collapsed into giggles. "They're fighting over the Celine Dion song from *Titanic!*"

The teacher finally managed to calm her would-be divas and resolved the standoff by giving each girl a different verse of the song to perform. The Leo fanatics reluctantly agreed. What else could they do?

By the time rehearsals were over, Morgan's head was ringing from having heard the hit song over and over and over in every variety of little girl voice imaginable. Leo might be adorable, but Morgan never wanted to watch *Titanic* again. She had heard the song "My Heart Will Go On" enough times to last a lifetime.

# Kristin

## Good-bye, Chicago. Hello, Laguna Beach

When Kristin's parents first broke the news that they were getting divorced she had been young and naïve enough to think the
idea was cool. Two of everything, she figured. Two houses, two
Christmases, two collections of Barbies. But what does an
eight-year-old know?

Things hadn't been so bad back when she and her brother
Mike were still living with their mom in Colorado. Dad had come
back almost every weekend to be with them. But now that he
and Mike were living in Laguna Beach and Kristin had been
forced to move to Chicago with her mom and her mom's new
husband, things were going from bad to worse.

At first Kristin had hoped it would all work out. She could
deal with moving to a new place. She had already lived in Con-
necticut and Colorado. And she genuinely wanted the best for
her mom. She still remembered how happy Mom looked during
the small wedding ceremony beside the pool in the backyard of
their new house in Chicago. Her stepdad was a good guy, too.
She got along with him just fine.

But her stepbrother and stepsister were impossible to live
with. And it didn't help that Mom kept trying to play peacemaker
instead of taking her side. Kristin was miserable. As an eighth
grader, her only recourse was to try and stay out of it as much as
possible.

Sometimes that meant staying at a friend's house. Sometimes it meant sneaking out just to get away. She had gotten

caught more than once, and she knew her mom was reaching the end of her patience. Kristin had heard her on the phone complaining to her dad in California that Kristin was getting hard to handle. "A real handful," she'd say. Mom's newest tactic was to threaten her by saying, "The next time you get in trouble, you're moving to California to live with your dad!"

"Fine," Kristin would tell her. She'd been to Laguna. It was gorgeous. "I *want* to move to California!"

But her mom never sent her. She just kept threatening.

Then one night during the summer before ninth grade, Kristin asked her mom if she could sleep over at her friend Stephanie's house. Stephanie asked *her* mom if she could sleep over at Kristin's house.

Instead, the two girls hung out with friends and wandered around the neighborhood laughing and talking as the evening slipped away. They were still out at midnight (two hours past Kristin's curfew) when one of the moms decided to call the other to check up on them. Once they realized what had happened, they panicked and set out in their cars to find their missing daughters.

When Kristin's mom spotted her strolling along the sidewalk with Stephanie, she was beside herself with rage. Stephanie's mom grounded her, but for Kristin's mom grounding wasn't good enough.

"That's it!" she shouted. "I'm calling your father tomorrow. You're moving to Laguna Beach!"

This time she meant it. There was just one problem. Moving to Laguna Beach was hardly a punishment for Kristin. She couldn't wait.

# Stephen and Taylor

*Fire!*

Stephen knew something was wrong when his second-grade teacher hurried everyone out of the classroom five minutes before the bell was supposed to ring at the end of the day. As they filed into the hallway, they saw that it was already crowded with students whose teachers were shepherding them along to the exit as quickly as possible, too. The adults were all acting like everything was perfectly normal, but Stephen thought he could read worried looks on some of their faces.

He boarded the bus along with all the other kids from Top of the World Elementary School. Some of them were laughing and chattering as usual, psyched about being dismissed five minutes sooner than they'd expected. Others had their heads bent together, whispering about what might have happened to make school end early.

In a few minutes they knew exactly what had happened. And none of it was good.

As the bus rolled downhill, Stephen heard someone gasp. Then a kid screamed. He looked out the window and saw that the entire canyon across from the one they were descending was engulfed in flames. Fire was raging over the hillsides. Black ash was turning the normally blue sky dark and ominous, while the sun had turned a bizarre fiery orange, so intensely bright Stephen could hardly look at it.

By now many of the students on the bus were sobbing. A lot of them had noticed small fires on the way to school that morning but had given them little thought. Usually such blazes were controlled, used as practice by firefighters. But now they were watching their own neighborhoods go up in flames.

The driver took an unfamiliar route and pulled into the parking lot of the local high school. Anxious parents were already lined up at the curb, waiting to pick up their children. Stephen spotted his mom and dad in the crowd. He'd never been so grateful to see them.

After reassuring Stephen and his sister Lauren that their neighborhood of Bluebird Canyon was okay—at least for the time being—the family said little to each other on the ride home. When they drew near their own street, their fears intensified. What would they find? Would their house still be standing?

Stephen heaved a sigh of relief as his dad turned onto their street. There was his family's house. There were all his neighbors' houses. Most of their owners had spilled out onto the lawns and sidewalks and were staring in horror at the wildfire raging over a nearby canyon. A police cruiser with its lights flashing was driving up and down the block, instructing them all to evacuate as soon as possible. It was one of the most surreal sights of Stephen's life. Maybe the most surreal part of it was the fact that his neighbor Taylor was cheerfully jumping rope in the street in front of his house, as if she didn't have a care in the world.

Stephen shot her a puzzled look, then followed the rest of his family inside to pack their suitcases. They would spend the night at one of his mother's friend's houses outside the danger zone.

When Stephen reemerged from his house he glanced apprehensively at the burning canyon. The fire was so close he could actually see orange flames licking the hillside. The air felt hot and seemed filled with the smell of burning. To his amazement, Taylor was still in the street, rhythmically skipping over her jump rope.

Just then her father appeared in the doorway of her family's house. "Taylor!" he yelled. "You need to come home right away!"

Reluctantly she gathered up the rope, waved good-bye to Stephen, who was helping to hastily load the trunk, and skipped away. He piled into the backseat with his siblings and watched Taylor disappear into her own house as they drove away.

"I want you to pack a bag with everything you'll need for tonight," Taylor's dad instructed her calmly. "We won't be able to stay here. I wish your mother wasn't out of town. I'm not sure what to pack."

Taylor knew exactly what to pack. She grabbed the little suitcase her father handed her and made a beeline for her bedroom. There, sitting on the pretty floral bedspread atop her little wooden bed, were her prized possessions—her stuffed animals. She loaded them into her suitcase until it would barely close. There wasn't much room for clothes, but at least she'd saved the important things.

Taylor and her dad drove to her grandparents' house in South Laguna, a safe distance from the fires. On the way, she stared out the window at the strange-looking cars stuffed with everything people had managed to salvage. A vacuum cleaner dangled out of the back of one overstuffed trunk. The occupants inside the car looked panic-stricken.

All that night firefighters battled the blaze. By the next morning it was under control. Bluebird Canyon had survived. The air still carried an acrid, burnt smell, and ash was everywhere, black and grimy. (Years later, they would open seldom-used cabinets and ash would spill out.) But that didn't matter. Their houses were still standing. Stephen and Taylor and their families could go home again.

They would never forget the Laguna Beach fires. The frightening images from that day would be seared into their memories forever. For Stephen it would be the blinding, fiery orange sun against the blackened sky. For Taylor it would be the cars overflowing with jumbled possessions that people just like herself had managed to grab before being forced to abandon their homes, knowing they might never see them again.

# STEPHEN
## Hasta La Vista, Brother

Stephen was getting kicked out. For as long as he could remember, he'd shared a room with his big brother, John. Together they'd plastered the walls with surf posters and sports team pennants.

But now the bunk beds they had slept in forever were getting tossed out. Stephen felt a twinge of nostalgia, remembering the rows of numbers he had watched John draw and then cross out on the wooden planks that supported the top bunk as he counted down the last fifty days of school every year. He remembered all the nights he'd fallen asleep in the top bunk listening to the sound of John's voice drift up from somewhere below him in the darkness.

Stephen idolized his brother. Always had. So it was hard

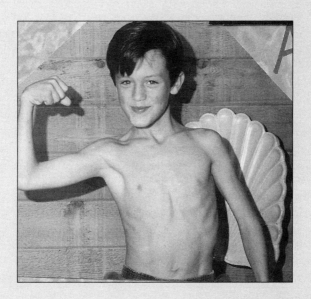

not to feel hurt by the fact that John no longer wanted him as a roommate. But lately they'd been fighting a lot. Everything Stephen did seemed to annoy John.

And Stephen understood. John was four years older. A high school guy needed his space. So Stephen, the seventh grader, set up camp downstairs in the den.

He soon got used to his new bedroom. He had to admit, having some privacy was kind of nice. Nobody told him what posters to put up on the walls, and he never had to deal with somebody else who wouldn't shut up or stop snoring long enough for him to fall asleep.

A few years later, when John headed off to college, Stephen moved back into their old bedroom. He took down John's decorations and covered the walls with shots of famous golf courses and, by the door, a collage of Jessica Simpson photos. (He *loved* Jessica.)

He would always have happy childhood memories of those many nighttime conversations with John, and of watching John cover every inch of wooden plank on the bed frame with his endless drawings. But Stephen wasn't too nostalgic these days. What teenager in his right mind wants to crawl up to the top bunk to crash every night? Stephen was a high school guy himself now. He needed his space.

# TREY

*Appetizers and More*

Trey couldn't believe the gorgeous, dark-haired girl from the catering staff was even bothering to give him the time of day. But there was no doubt about it, she was flirting with him as much as he was flirting with her. Whenever he could sneak a few minutes away from the endless waves of friends and relatives who'd shown up to celebrate his brother's engagement, all of whom seemed eager to talk his ear off, he'd sidle over and think of an excuse to strike up a conversation with her while she handed out hors d'oeuvres. He'd probably eaten more appetizers than anyone else at the party just to get close to the girl. He couldn't believe she was only a sophomore in high school—just a year older than he was.

Trey hardly considered himself a ladies' man, but at least he had finally outgrown his awkward chubster phase, and ditched the glasses and braces. He'd come a long way from the low point when he'd drawn a rose on a piece of paper, scribbled a poem next to it, and handed it to Lauren Conrad as a hopeful sixth grader, only to be shot down with a polite thanks-but-no-thanks. At least he was no longer too shy to talk to girls, and they weren't running in the opposite direction when he did.

Maybe it was the festive spirit of the night that buoyed his confidence. Maybe it was the fact that he was a freshman now, a bona fide high school kid. Whatever it was, something had somehow given him the courage to coax the pretty girl away from the crowd. And now, here he was face-to-face with her, talking quietly in a secluded corner, unnoticed by the dozens of adults just a stone's throw away.

Trey knew it was now or never. He had to go for it. He wasn't really sure he knew how to kiss (after all, he'd never done it), but he leaned in, closed his eyes . . . and she didn't pull away. Instead, she kissed him back. And she kept kissing him, while the conversation and the candlelight and the laughter from the party washed over them.

Later that night, lying in bed and reliving the evening, Trey would remember it as a total out-of-body experience. And though he never dated the girl, never asked her to prom or got asked to winter formal by her, he would remember the special moment they shared together that night for years to come.

# TREY
## No Vampires, Please

It's just a movie. It's not even supposed to be scary. That's what six-year-old Trey kept telling himself as he sat huddled between his four older brothers and sisters in the darkened theater. So far, he wasn't convincing himself at all.

Treating the family to a movie night of *Buffy the Vampire Slayer* while vacationing in Maui seemed like a great idea to Trey's parents, sitting several rows behind their kids. But, of course, they had no idea their youngest son was close to hyperventilating into his bucket of popcorn.

It's a *movie*, Trey told himself again, trying to calm his racing heart. Just a stupid movie. But when yet another gruesome, fanged image flashed onscreen he gave in to his fears. The thought of some evil creature sinking its teeth into his neck and stealing his blood was just about the worst thing he could imagine. Too spellbound to take his eyes off the film but too terrified to sit still any longer, he stood up and began edging his way down the row of seats, bumping into strangers' knees and tripping over their feet.

At last he reached the aisle and, with his eyes still glued on Buffy's every move, he began carefully backing up in the dark, counting each aisle as he passed. One . . . two . . . Mom and Dad were sitting three rows behind. Weren't they?

It would have been easier to see where he was going if he could have wrenched his gaze away from those larger-than-life-size vampires, but, petrified though he was, he was still dying to find out what happened next.

At last Trey worked his way back three rows, slipped past a

man in the aisle seat, and crept along to the middle, where he was sure his mother was sitting.

"This movie is a lot scarier than I thought it would be. Is it okay if I sit here?" he whispered as he sank gratefully onto her lap.

"What's that, honey?" asked an unfamiliar voice.

Horrified, Trey whipped around and saw a strange woman peering at him in the dark. She looked just as shocked to find a kid on her lap as Trey felt to be sitting there.

"Trey?" Mrs. Phillips's voice floated up from a nearby row. "Is that you?"

Mortified, Trey leapt off the strange woman's lap, hurried to the aisle, and back to the next row, where he collapsed in the empty seat next to his mom.

As his heart gradually stopped flopping like a fish and returned to a normal pace, Trey had to admit that, though it wasn't how he'd planned to conquer his fear of horror films, finding himself on that stranger's lap had taken the fright right out of *Buffy the Vampire Slayer*.

Young Kristin in high chair.

Young Stephen, baseball star.

Taylor and her dad on the high seas.

Jason shows off his catch.

No. 101

Lauren takes Disneyland by storm.

BILLABONG

Talan was always a cutie!

Dieter, Stephen, and Trey—pals for life.

Jessica looking sweet in a Christmas dress.

Jen and Lauren purge their pores.

They're with the band—
Can you spot Stephen,
Dieter, and Alex M.?

Jason, Cedric,
Alex M., and Taylor
with friend Emily.

Morgan S., Alex M., and Alex H., dressed up in junior high.

Jen, Lauren, and Lo.

Stephen and Kristin
goofing around.

Stephen and Lauren
on Lauren's birthday.

Talan and Christina
looking glam.

Dieter and Jessica with
Jessica's mom and sister.

Christina and Lo.

Kristin and Jason in earlier days.

Alex M., Morgan, Kristin, Alex H., and Christina.

Stephen and Dieter.

Jessica and Taylor.

Lo, Lauren, and Jen, hanging around.

Jessica and Kristin.
Don't take pictures
and drive, kids!

Taylor and Talan.

Taylor, Alex M., and Morgan S.

Kristin, Alex M., and Morgan S., at a Halloween party.

Stephen and Kristin at prom.

Careful, your face might freeze that way: Alex H. and Kristin.

Friends forever. Taylor and Alex M.

Alex H., Taylor, Kristin, and Morgan S.

Jason and Alex M. at winter formal.

Spring Break!

Sun worshipping in Cabo.

Talan gets some love in Cabo.

Cedric is one lucky guy.

Stephen, Lauren, Trey, and Dieter in San Francisco.

# LAUREN

## Sweet Sixteen at Last

It might have been a stupid rule, but there was no getting around it. Lauren wasn't allowed to date until she turned sixteen. And if you couldn't date, what was the use of having a boyfriend?

Besides, she didn't want to miss out on all the fun of being with her girlfriends during her sophomore year. They always had such a great time together. And, hey, she figured, there were plenty of cute guys around to hook up with at parties if you just needed someone to kiss. Boyfriends? Serious dating? Definitely *not* high on the priority list.

So when she and Christina were hanging out at Lo's house one night and Lo asked if they wanted to visit the guy who lived next door, a senior at their high school, Lauren said, "Sure."

It turned out several other senior guys were already at Lo's neighbor's house watching TV with him. Lauren didn't know any of them, though she recognized a boy named Dane because he was the senior class president. Lauren was the sophomore class president, and they had been in a leadership class together at school, despite their age difference. Dane recognized Lauren, too, and before she knew it they had struck up a conversation. By the end of the night, they were holding hands and exchanging phone numbers.

"So," Lo asked, suppressing a giggle, as they walked back to her house. "What's up with you and Dane?"

"I don't know." Lauren shrugged. "He seems nice."

Dane called the next day. And the next. Before long they

were together all the time. Things always happen when you're not looking for them, and in spite of her best intentions, Lauren had a boyfriend . . . a boyfriend who she couldn't date because her sixteenth birthday was still a whole six months away. It might as well have been forever.

She couldn't bring herself to fess up about being under the legal limit for dating in the Conrad house. Not when Dane was a senior with a driver's license, a car, and probably a free pass from his parents to date as much as he wanted. So, instead she started coming up with creative excuses to keep him from catching on to the fact that she wasn't allowed to go anywhere alone with him.

If Dane wanted to drive her to a party, Lauren would tell him Lo or Christina had already begged her to go with them. Why didn't she just meet him there instead? If he showed up at her house to watch movies while her parents were supposedly going out to dinner, she was ready with a story about how one of them wasn't feeling well so they had decided to stay home at the last minute.

Dane accepted her stories without question. Either he genuinely believed them or he didn't want to embarrass her. All the same, Lauren was relieved when at last her sixteenth birthday arrived. She was running out of ideas for cover stories.

Her girlfriends took her out for sushi in honor of the big

night. Right in the middle of dinner, the waitress brought over an enormous bouquet of roses from Dane. Attached to it was a note offering to take her out for a special birthday dinner, just the two of them.

A few nights later, Dane picked Lauren up at her front door with no objection from her or her parents and drove her to an elegant restaurant, where they were seated at the best table in the house and treated to a delicious meal topped off with a sinfully rich dessert. As they drove home, Lauren thanked her boyfriend for an amazing evening.

"I wanted to do something special to celebrate," he told her. "I wanted to make sure it was a memorable date."

"Don't worry," Lauren assured him. "It was."

# Taylor
## T'n' T

Taylor still remembered the huge crush she'd had on Tyler when she first met him the summer before her freshman year. He was tall, dark, handsome, and two years older, which made him even hotter. At the time she had been dating his friend Andrew, and breaking the news to him had been pretty bad, but Taylor and Tyler had been together ever since.

They were one of Laguna's longest-lasting high school couples, a fixture at parties and dances. She had never even been to a winter formal or a prom without him. All the guys knew Taylor was Tyler's girlfriend. They wouldn't touch her with a ten-foot pole even if they wanted to. Gossip got around in the Bubble, and nobody wanted to make Tyler mad.

But now Tyler was graduating and going off to college in another state, and Taylor would be left at home. She tried to act enthusiastic for him. She even helped him pack. But though Tyler assured her they would stay together and promised to call every day, Taylor was still going to be stuck in Laguna without him. She hadn't technically spent a single day of high school without a boyfriend. She had no idea what to expect, but she had a sneaking suspicion it might suck.

She was still bummed when junior year started. She moped around at home for a few weeks, then decided she might as well go out and be depressed rather than stay home and do nothing and be depressed. Her family had just moved into a bigger house, and her parents had bought her an Acura Integra. New house. New car. Why not a new start?

So she began spending more time with Alex M. and her other girlfriends. They went shopping, they went out to lunch, and they got ready for parties at one another's houses. Sometimes they just hung out. Taylor couldn't believe she had been missing out on so much fun by spending all her time with a boyfriend.

Sure, she was looking forward to seeing Tyler when he came home at Thanksgiving, and she still beamed when he assured her, "I'm not looking for another girl. I'm not interested in anyone else." But this time saying good-bye afterward wasn't so painful.

In fact, Taylor was stoked to get back to the girls. She was even stoked on going to winter formal without a guy so that she could spend more time with her friends.

Which was a good thing because all the guys still thought of Taylor as Tyler's girlfriend, and none of them would touch her with a ten-foot pole, even if they wanted to. After all, gossip got around in the Bubble, and nobody wanted to make Tyler mad.

# Taylor
## Oh, Baby

Taylor had wanted a little brother or sister for as long as she could remember. So, when she was fifteen and she heard the news that she was at last getting her wish, she thought her mother was joking.

But watching her mom suffer through morning sickness, mood swings, cravings, and swollen feet wasn't what she had bargained for. It was enough to make Taylor feel almost like she was suffering through it herself. "Seeing this is the best birth control you could ever think of, isn't it?" her mom said wryly one morning as she eased herself uncomfortably onto a chair. Taylor had to agree. By the end of nine months she was exhausted.

And that was just the beginning. Taylor adored her baby brother, Brook, from the moment she first saw him, but the diapers, the spit-ups, and the sleepless nights for the whole family

were endless. High school textbooks were a piece of cake compared to some of the stuff in those baby care books.

Still, Taylor adored Brook. By the time she was a senior in high school and he was a toddler, old enough to talk, she felt more like a second mom to him than a sister. Sometimes she couldn't resist asking him, "Brook, do you love me?"

In typical defiant toddler fashion, he would cross his arms and pout and say, "No! I don't!" especially if Taylor was trying to coax him into doing something he didn't want to do, like eating vegetables or getting ready for bed.

"Yes, you do! You love me!" Taylor would tease.

"No!"

Their mother, unable to believe she was witnessing a sibling squabble between an eighteen-year-old and a three-year-old, would just shake her head, unsure whether to laugh at them or scold them.

"Admit it! You *do* love me," Taylor would whisper as soon as her mom was out of earshot.

Inevitably, Brook would beam at her. "Yes," he would say. "I love you, Taylor."

# TALAN

## Surfing with Sharks

Talan couldn't help noticing the long, jagged scars on the leg of the charter boat operator as he and his friend Mike clambered onboard with their surfboards for the trip to Witch's Rock. Located off the coast of Costa Rica, the jagged rock formation was said to have some of the best surfing in the world. The fifteen-

year-olds had come all the way down from Laguna with Talan's dad to see for themselves whether it lived up to its rep.

But the waters were also said to be shark-infested, and crocodiles reportedly lived in the fast-flowing river that emptied into the ocean nearby. You'd better know what you were doing on a surfboard if you wanted to ride the waves off Witch's Rock, and if you got in trouble you'd better remember to head back to the boat—never toward land and the riverbank, where a croc might be lying in wait, hidden in the lush jungle vegetation of the rainforest.

Talan nudged Mike and pointed at the man's scar. It definitely looked like a vicious bite mark that had long since healed over.

"That's some scar," said Talan. "Is it from a shark or a crocodile?"

"This?" said the man, glancing down casually. "Naw. I got this motorcycle riding."

Just then Witch's Rock loomed into view, jutting sharply skyward out of the blue waters. It was beyond beautiful, and the waves looked incredible. The break was perfect. The captain parked the boat about two hundred yards offshore and in moments, Talan and Mike were paddling in, through the eighty-degree water, to enjoy some of the best surfing they'd ever experienced.

Back on the boat at the end of the day, Talan couldn't resist asking about the scar one more time.

"Hey," he said to the captain. "Tell me the truth. Did you really get that scar in a motorcycle accident?"

The man chuckled. "Kid," he said, "I run a charter boat for surfers. If I'd told you I got this in the water off Witch's Rock, would you have hired me to take you surfing there?"

Talan and Mike had to agree. Safe onboard the boat once again, staring out at the incredible waves and shimmering waters, it was easier to laugh about the idea than it would have been a few hours earlier.

"So, what's it from?" Talan asked. "A shark? A crocodile?"

The man shrugged and continued to guide the boat back toward the mainland. "Coulda been a shark. Coulda been a crocodile. Who knows? I was paddling in and something bit me in the water off Witch's Rock."

# KRISTIN

## *Best Friends Are Formed*

Kristin wasn't thrilled with her dad's decision to send her to Catholic school for her freshman year in Laguna Beach. First, her family wasn't even Catholic. Second, the school was forty-five minutes away, which meant she had to get up extra early every morning and she got home so late after school that she missed a ton of prime after-school beach time.

At least it was better than having to stay in frigid, windy Chicago with her stepsiblings, Kristin told herself. Besides, the uniforms weren't bad, some of the kids actually seemed pretty nice, and she could always hang out at the beach on the weekends.

Since Santa Margarita High School didn't offer driver's education, Kristin had to take the class in the evening at the local public high school instead. She was used to being the new girl by now. She knew she might have to sit by herself for the entire course, but so what? She could deal. It's just one class, she reminded herself as she walked down a hallway of the school. She found the room number she was looking for and braced herself to see a room full of unfamiliar and possibly unfriendly faces as she walked into driver's ed on the first night of class.

It wasn't what she expected at all. Almost from the moment she sat down, she was struck by how warm and friendly everybody was. Somehow she just hit it off with the other kids in class. They seemed much more like her than the students at her own school. First she met a guy named Ian. He introduced her to a girl named Alex M.

Alex, who knew how closed the Bubble could seem to outsiders, always made it a point to help newcomers feel welcome, especially newcomers like Kristin. Alex liked her instantly.

"We should hang out sometime," Alex said casually one night as they were walking out of class together. "Gimme a call."

Kristin thought about it after she got home. Girls said things like that all the time and they didn't mean it. They didn't really expect you to call. But, why not? Alex seemed genuine, and Kristin was anxious to make some new friends outside Santa Margarita.

Alex sounded a little surprised to hear Kristin's voice, but

she warmed up quickly and invited Kristin to a party a guy named Talan was throwing a few nights later.

"What's his name?" Kristin asked, thinking she might have misunderstood.

"Talan," Alex repeated. "He's nice. A lot of the girls think he's hot. Actually, he's probably hooked up with half of them already," she added with a laugh.

Kristin eagerly agreed to go to Talan's party with Alex M. that Friday night. To her delight, Alex knew everyone, and before long, so did Kristin. Just as in driver's ed, Kristin was impressed by how easily she fit in with the kids from the public high school. She especially liked a girl named Alex H., who she'd met that night.

"Kristin's a lot of fun," Alex H. told Alex M. "How come we've never met her before?"

"She goes to Catholic school," Alex M. told her. "But I'm pretty sure she wants to switch and go to school with us next year."

In no time at all, Kristin and the two Alexes were the best of friends. They went everywhere together—to lunch, to the beach, to parties. They were too young to drive, so when they wanted to go anyplace that was too far to walk, they took the bus. It didn't matter where A.K.A.—as they called themselves—went, they always had fun. Something happened nearly every day to send them into fits of hysterical laughter, whether it was a guy's lame pickup line or Kristin's goofy Brady Bunch dance.

When Kristin finished driver's ed, she was sure she had failed her permit test because she got nine wrong (you were only allowed to miss seven), and her road test because she ran over a curb (an automatic fail). But she didn't care. She was happy in Laguna Beach. She had a new life and new friends. Really good friends. Hopefully they would do better than she did on the road test and once they had driver's licenses they would be able to give her rides. If not, she'd take the bus.

Who cared? At least she had parties to go to now.

To her amazement, the guys who administered the driving tests let her slide. They gave her passing grades despite her mistakes. Life was good.

And it was about to get even better. Kristin's dad agreed to let her attend the public high school, with the two Alexes and all her other friends, starting in the fall of her sophomore year.

# STEPHEN

### The New Girl

Stephen and his friend Connor watched the blonde girl walk across the quad at lunch.

Connor nudged Stephen. "I've never seen *her* before. Who is she?"

"She just started going to our school," Stephen answered. "Her name's Kristin. I've played golf with her older brother Mike."

"She's pretty cute," said Connor.

"Yeah," Stephen agreed. "But I think she's got a boyfriend."

"Figures." Connor looked dejected. "Well, you already get enough girls. If it turns out she doesn't have a boyfriend, you've gotta leave her for me."

"We'll see," said Stephen, smiling.

# KRISTIN AND STEPHEN

## A Trip to Knott's Berry Farm

"I kinda think I like Connor," Kristin confessed to her friend Alex H. one afternoon while they were hanging out at Alex's house after school.

"Really?" Alex asked her. "Let me see what I can do."

The next thing Kristin knew, Alex was on the phone with Connor's friend Stephen making plans for the four of them to go to Knott's Berry Farm amusement park that weekend. Alex and Stephen were old friends, but Kristin only knew him a little. She thought he must be a pretty nice guy, though, if he was willing to help Connor out. He even offered to drive.

Stephen and Connor picked the girls up at their houses Saturday morning and headed north to Knott's Berry Farm, where they spent the day enjoying the rides. Stephen kept them laughing the whole afternoon. He was a little hyper, but he was hilarious. And he's hot, thought Kristin.

Connor was nice. He was cute. But as the day wore on Kristin found herself wanting to sit next to Stephen on the roller coasters more than she wanted to sit next to Connor.

Maybe word had never reached Connor that this was supposed to be a setup. Maybe he wasn't even interested. Anyway, it wasn't like anything had actually happened between them.

When they got back to Laguna Beach that night, Kristin and Alex told the guys good night and watched them drive away.

Kristin turned to her friend. "I kinda think I like Stephen," she said.

# STEPHEN AND KRISTIN
## The First Date

Connor was a pretty shy guy, so when Stephen heard from Alex H. that the new girl, Kristin, liked him, Stephen did his best to help Connor out. Stephen was as surprised as anyone when the rumor reached him through Laguna Beach's never-ending gossip chain that Kristin had changed her mind. She liked *him* instead.

Connor didn't know Kristin well enough to be truly mad about the situation, so Stephen decided he might as well go for it. He figured he must have gotten a lot better at asking girls out over the years, because Kristin agreed to have dinner with him that Friday night at everybody's favorite sushi restaurant, San Shi Go.

• • •

Stephen couldn't believe how nervous he was on his first date with Kristin. He knew he was talking a mile a minute. She just kept sitting there and nodding, probably because she couldn't manage to get a word in edgewise. Worse, he had dropped his chopsticks at least half a dozen times already. He didn't even know how to use them, but he didn't want Kristin to know he was that unsophisticated.

Kristin smiled at Stephen as she fumbled with her chopsticks. Why did she have so many butterflies in her stomach? She hadn't felt this way at all at Knott's Berry Farm. She was grateful that her date seemed to be having no problem keeping up a nonstop stream of nervous conversation all by himself. He hadn't stopped talking since they sat down, so maybe he wouldn't notice how nervous she was. But the chopsticks were a telltale sign. She had never learned to use the stupid things and now her hands were so unsteady that the sushi kept falling back onto her plate.

When one of the chopsticks finally slipped out of her fingers and fell to the floor with a clatter, Stephen stopped talking long enough to catch his breath.

"Sorry," said Kristin. "What were you saying?"

"Do you want me to get you a new pair of chopsticks?" Stephen asked politely, starting to flag down a waiter.

"No." Kristin shook her head. "Actually, I can't get the hang of them. I normally just use a fork."

Stephen grinned. "Me, too," he said, tossing his chopsticks down on the table and reaching for his fork. "I was just trying to impress you."

Kristin didn't say so, but he had succeeded. Stephen definitely impressed her.

# KRISTIN

## *Grounded!*

By now, Kristin was an expert at sneaking out of her house. She'd been doing it ever since junior high back in Chicago. And at her dad's house in Laguna Beach her bedroom was on the ground floor, which meant sneaking out was almost too easy. All you had to do was open the window and hop out.

Most of the time Kristin got away with it. Even the night when she and Alex H. and Alex M. all came tumbling in through her bedroom window after a party, and somebody stepped on the blow-dryer Kristin had left lying on the floor. The dryer went off—on the "high" setting, naturally— sending a piercing mechanical whine through

the quiet house before they could find the buttons and figure out which one to press to shut it off. Amazingly, neither the dryer nor their stifled giggles woke anybody up.

Of course, once in a while Kristin would come home to find the window locked. That meant she had to either sleep outside (not an option) or go around to the front door and knock so that whoever had realized she was gone and decided to lock her out could open the door for her and then let her know how much trouble she was in. Most of the time, Kristin had to admit her dad and her stepmom were pretty reasonable.

She felt a little guilty about lying to them tonight, but she had just started dating Stephen and she really wanted to hang out with him. It was a school night, though, and there was no way they would go for it.

She couldn't very well make up an excuse to go to bed superearly and then sneak out the window, either. Nobody would believe her. So she told her dad she had to work at her hostessing job at the seafood restaurant down the street. She often didn't get home from work before 11:00 P.M. even on week-nights, so she'd be covered.

When she met Stephen that evening she had every intention of getting home by 11:00. But they were having so much fun that time just slipped away. Neither one of them realized it.

By about 11:15, Kristin's dad was getting worried. At 11:30, he finally called the restaurant to see why his daughter was working so late and to make sure everything was okay.

"You're looking for Kristin?" asked a puzzled voice on the other end of the line. "She's not working tonight."

Kristin's dad immediately jumped in the car and drove off to look for her. He was overwhelmed with relief when he found her a few blocks away, sitting and talking with Stephen in the front seat of his car.

"Uh-oh," Kristin said, catching sight of her father's angry face as he slammed the car door and stalked over. She remembered all too well what happened the last time she got caught out after her curfew and one of her parents showed up in a car looking for her.

"Dad," Kristin stammered, getting out of the car. "I'm really sorry."

"Kristin," he said sternly, his face a mixture of anger and relief at finding her unharmed.

She held her breath waiting for the punishment.

"You are *grounded,*" he told her firmly. "For the next two weeks!"

Kristin let out a sigh of relief. She gave Stephen a quick wave good-bye, then walked obediently over to her dad's car. She could deal with being stuck at home for fourteen days. As long as her dad didn't threaten to send her back to Chicago, she wasn't complaining.

# KRISTIN
## The Barbie Massacre

Kristin *loved* Barbie dolls. Of all her toys, they were her favorites—even better than Beanie Babies. By age five, she had a whole collection of them, and, like lots of other little girls, she spent hours dressing them up and sending them off on imaginary adventures.

Kristin's Barbies were right in the middle of just such an adventure one afternoon in her family's living room. But just as things were getting exciting, Kristin's relatives showed up, and she had to leave the Barbies where they were, planning to go back to them later that day.

Her cousins Danny and Jimmy bounded off to play with her older brother, Mike, as soon as they walked into the house, which left Kristin to hang out with her aunt, her uncle, and her parents. Not that she minded. Her aunt and uncle were really nice. But she was still eager to get back to her Barbies.

As soon as she figured she had put in enough time with the grown-ups to be polite, Kristin excused herself and raced back to the living room in search of her Barbies. She reached the doorway and . . . Oh no! Kristin wasn't sure whether to scream or cry at the scene in front of her.

There were Danny, Jimmy, and Mike holding baseball bats and wearing guilty expressions. All around their feet lay the bodies of mutilated Barbie dolls. There were Barbies with bashed-in faces. Barbies with missing arms and legs. Little bits of her beloved dolls were scattered all over the rug. There wasn't one undamaged Barbie left.

"DAAAAAAAAAAAD!!!!!!" Kristin yelled at the top of her lungs.

The boys cringed. Barbie baseball had seemed like a really good idea at the time, but suddenly they had a sneaking suspicion their parents might not see it that way. At the sounds of hurried adult footsteps approaching, Mike's eyes widened in fear. The cousins glanced around wildly for an escape route. Too late.

They were caught red-handed. A Barbie's head still dangled from Mike's fist, her long blonde hair twisted around his fingers, ready for the windup.

Kristin's aunt did her best to calm her down. Then she forced the boys to mumble an apology. "Don't worry," she assured Kristin. "I'll make them all buy you new Barbie dolls." Kristin hung her head and nodded.

"Okay," she said. "Thank you."

The three new Barbie dolls that arrived were better than nothing, but they didn't make up for the loss of the originals. They were just a starter kit, as far as Kristin was concerned. Her stupid brother and cousins had murdered more than ten of her precious Barbies.

Still, the thought of Mike, Danny, and Jimmy being forced to pass up the cool Ninja Turtles stuff in the toy store because they knew they had to spend their money on Barbie dolls instead made her feel a little better. She could just picture them shuffling reluctantly up to the counter under the watchful eye of her aunt, each clutching a Barbie. She wished she could have seen the looks on their faces when the salesgirl saw what they were buying.

# KRISTIN

## The Midnight Invitation

"What the . . ."

Kristin fumbled for her cell phone in the dark. Who would be calling in the middle of the night on a school night? Still half-asleep, she sat up in bed, switched on the light by her bed, and saw that there was a new text message on her phone.

GO TO THE WINDOW, it read.

It was probably someone Kristin knew playing a joke. Then again, there was something unsettling about an anonymous message waking you out of a sound sleep. And her bedroom was on the first floor. What if some creepy guy from her sopho-more class had found out her number and now he was standing right outside her window leering in? She couldn't even remem-ber if she had locked it or not.

Kristin hesitated, but then her curiosity got the better of her, and she tiptoed over to the window. She reached for the curtains and pulled them back just a crack, just far enough to peek out. When she saw what was waiting outside, a huge smile broke over her face.

Dozens of little glowing white candles were burning brightly on the lawn, all set up to spell out letters followed by a question mark. In the flickering, dancing candlelight, she could see Stephen standing next to them, holding a bouquet of roses and looking hopefully at her window.

Kristin tugged on the bottom of the sash and raised the win-dow enough to lean out as Stephen hurried over.

"Oh my God!" she squealed. "I can't believe you did this! YES! Of course I'll go to prom with you!"

# STepHEN ANd DiETER

*Stanley Goes Cruising*

Outsiders always assumed Laguna Beach kids were pampered and privileged, but Dieter wondered what they would think if they saw him today. He was exhausted from his daytime summer job as a rep for a dog food company, his muscles were torn and cramped from grueling practices to gear up for the coming soccer season, and now he was heading off to his night job supervising the grounds crew at the annual Sawdust arts festival.

The festival job was fun for Dieter 99 percent of the time because he got to work with his friends. (So many Laguna Beach teenagers worked the Sawdust that it was like a rite of passage in the Bubble.) The only time the job sucked was when he occasionally had to fire a friend for slacking off. Dieter hated to fire anyone, but you couldn't have one guy getting paid to hang out with all the girls who worked the soft drink stand while everyone else on the grounds crew picked up his share of the trash.

For Dieter, the best part of working was being able to buy things he really wanted with his own money. Today was a special occasion because he had finally managed to save up enough to buy what he wanted most: a car.

Okay, so it wasn't his dream car. (Someday he'd have enough for a Ford Explorer.) But it was the next best thing: a black 1987 Lincoln Mark VII with leather seats. With his wallet $3,000 lighter, Dieter cruised out of the lot in his new prize possession. The engine sounded like it was ready to explode. Actually, it sounded more like a lawnmower than a car. But, so what? He would be able to start sophomore year with his own ride.

Stephen almost fell over laughing when he caught sight of Dieter behind the wheel.

"You look like you're straight out of Compton," he said, fighting back tears of laughter. "What were you thinking? That's no car for a little white boy like you."

"I like it," said Dieter, defensively. "Do you want a ride or not?"

Stephen hopped in. "Oh, man," he said, running a hand over the leather interior to inspect it. "We have *got* to give this car a name!"

Stanley, as they nicknamed the Lincoln, soon became a fixture in their lives and the source of numerous adventures. It didn't take long before everyone at school recognized the sound of Dieter's deafening engine and knew Stanley was grinding its way into the parking lot. (Later, when Jessica and Dieter started dating, she was so mortified by the car that she had to fight the urge to force her boyfriend to choose between her and Stanley.)

On weekends, it sometimes seemed like Dieter and Stephen couldn't take Stanley out for more than ten minutes without the police pulling them over. First they would hear the telltale whine of the siren and see the flashing lights behind them. Then Dieter would obediently slow down and pull Stanley over to the curb. Amused, he would watch the officer get out of the patrol car and saunter up to the driver's side.

Inevitably, the cop would lean down to peer in the window and then do a double take. Dieter would sneak a grin at Stephen. They knew precisely what the guy was thinking: You're two little white boys from Laguna Beach. What are you doing driving around in a car that looks like it's straight out of Compton?

Stanley's most bizarre and frightening trick was that every so often its steering would lock up and simply refuse to work. On two occasions, Dieter had no choice but to watch in dry-mouthed horror as his car hurtled toward whatever was directly in its path and inevitably crashed into it with a shuddering crunch. Both times it happened he got lucky: He wasn't driving fast and there were no other cars around; he hit walls instead.

Then one day toward the end of junior year as Dieter headed for the Green Bridge, which would soon be home to numerous prom invitation banners, Stanley did it again. Dieter wrenched the wheel frantically to the right, then to the left, but the car ignored him as if it had a mind of its own and made straight for one of the bridge's supporting walls. Dieter gripped the useless steering wheel and sat there as the wall got closer and closer and . . . *crash!!!*

A few minutes later, as a pale and shaking Dieter climbed out and reached for the cell phone to call his father, he looked ruefully down at the car. "That's it, Stanley," he said. "I'm over this. I don't wanna die."

The Lincoln had given Dieter and Stephen a lot of great memories, but Dieter had at last saved enough to buy his fantasy Ford Explorer. Besides, he'd had about all he could take of Stanley's antics. He happily sold the car for $1,000, advised the new owner to get the steering fixed, and wished him good luck as he drove away.

# Stephen and Dieter

## *Busted!*

"I'm still hungry. Are you?"

It was the night before soccer playoffs were due to start in his junior year, and Dieter was starving. Maybe it was nerves. He and Stephen had just picked up a bag full of fast food and wolfed it down back at home. He knew he had a big game coming up. He should probably be home getting some sleep, but he felt like he could down about three more orders of fries.

"Let's go back and get some more," Stephen suggested.

So they climbed into the car again and retraced their route to the fast-food restaurant.

They were sitting in the front seat in the parking lot, speculating about the team's chances in the upcoming match and wondering whether the guy at the drive-thru had realized this was their second meal in about twenty minutes, when the wail of police sirens drowned out their conversation. The noise was so deafening, Dieter and Stephen figured the police cars must be driving right past the parking lot on their way to the scene of a crime.

"I wonder what happened," Dieter said absently, between bites.

The next thing they knew, there were flashing lights all around them. They peered curiously out the window and found that police cruisers had pulled up on either side of their car. They squinted as the blinding beam of a flashlight was pointed into the front seat. Behind it they could see an officer staring in at them suspiciously.

"Did you do it?!" he demanded.

"Huh?" Since when was it against the law to eat a second order of fries?

"Somebody made a prank call to 911 from the payphone right over there," the officer said, pointing to a payphone at the edge of the parking lot. "There's nobody else here but you."

"What?!" Stephen exclaimed, noticing the payphone for the first time. "No way!"

"You kids think this is funny?" the first officer demanded angrily. "Making prank calls to 911 is no joke, son."

"We didn't call anyone!" Dieter insisted.

The officer moved his light to Dieter's face.

"We were just sitting here eating," Dieter insisted. "We didn't even get out of the car."

The officer scrutinized him. "Hey," he said suddenly. "Don't you play for Andy?"

"Excuse me?"

"Don't you play soccer for Andy, the coach at the high school?"

Dieter nodded, puzzled.

Suddenly the officer relaxed. His tone sounded calm, even friendly. "What are you doing out so late?" he asked. "You should be home getting some sleep. You've got a big game coming up, you know."

# TREY

## Protesting in Paris

Adjusting to life in Paris wasn't easy for Trey. When his parents asked one day while they drove the family minivan along the California coast if he'd like to spend his sophomore year of high school in France, Trey had blurted out "Sure!" almost before they finished the question. He'd already spent six months of fourth grade attending school in Costa Rica and more than a year of junior high in San Francisco. He was willing to bet Paris would be even cooler.

But things had gone wrong from the start. First, his parents had insisted on moving in the middle of summer, tearing Trey away from his friends and a girl he really liked. For a family that never argued, they sure had done a lot of it since they'd moved to Paris.

Next there was the language barrier. Trey was trying his best, but Parisians seemed to have a major lack of patience when it came to dealing with an American teenager stumbling over *s'il vous plait* and other basic phrases.

Then school had started, and talk about tough. Even though it was an international school with kids from all over the world, the teachers enforced the French-*only* speaking policy with a vengeance and they had no qualms about yelling at you in front of your classmates if you did something wrong. (Getting yelled at, Trey discovered, sucked even if you weren't quite sure what the person was yelling about.) Worse, there were no organized sports and the challenging classes dragged on until it was dark outside in the winter.

Trey and his new best friend, a Danish kid named Thomas, got used to joking about how bad their French was and grinning furtively at each other when they got reprimanded for giving the wrong answer. That made school more bearable. And hearing from Stephen helped, too. As always, the two close friends kept in touch. In fact, Stephen and another friend of theirs named Jonathan were planning to fly over for a visit in the spring, which gave Trey something to look forward to.

At least there were some upsides to life in Paris. There were great museums like the Louvre, just a short walk from their house. Trey loved the former palace, and he frequently wandered through it with his mom, admiring the immense collection of famous artworks.

Parisian fashions, too, were amazing. Looking in the shop windows and watching the well-dressed people strolling along the boulevards was almost as good as the museum, scenery-wise.

Trey had always had his own unique sense of style when it came to clothes. (He credited it to the Scottish nanny who had taken care of him years earlier and dressed him in plaid pants and neon socks while the other little kids ran around in boring T-shirts and jeans.) He'd gotten harassed for it more than once back in California, but he'd never let that discourage him. Here the art and fashion fueled his imagination more than ever, and he found himself coming up with ideas for his own designs, then sketching them out in his spare time, just as he had once done with his soccer uniforms. Hats were his new favorites when it came to design.

Maybe it was because there were no sports around to distract them, but Trey couldn't get over how focused everyone was on academics here. The teachers were tough, but they seemed to love their jobs and to care about making sure students learned. Just as they didn't hold back when they were mad at you, they didn't hold back about voicing their opinions. And they had opinions about *everything*.

Growing up in the Phillips house, politics had always been

something to chat about at the dinner table. *Did you hear what happened in Afghanistan yesterday? What do you think of it? Oh, and please pass the potatoes.* Trey knew that a highly controversial politician with some radical ideas was running for president, and that his speeches scared a lot of people. But he was still stunned when he strolled into class one day and his teacher demanded to know, "What are you doing here?"

"Don't we have school today?" he asked innocently.

"Why aren't you at the political rally? Don't you care what happens in the election?" The teacher directed the question not just to Trey, but to all the students who had shown up. "Allez-y!" The teacher told them. "Go!"

Trey didn't need another excuse to get out of class. He jumped up and took the Métro to the center of Paris with some of his friends, where the rally was in full swing. When he stepped out of the station, his jaw dropped open. He was surrounded by the biggest crowd he'd ever seen. There were people, throngs of them, everywhere. Many weren't much older than Trey. In moments he was swept up in the energetic crowd. Was he going to be trampled? Arrested? He glanced around for an escape route, but to his amazement he realized that this was no angry mob stomping through the street. Nobody was scowling or shouting. The vibe was totally positive. There were brightly colored balloons and trucks with bands playing music and people were singing along. Sure, the songs were political—and they were in French—but they were upbeat and happy. People were dancing. Everyone was smiling. *This* was a political rally? It was empowering. It was *fun.*

That night Trey practically burst through the door in his eagerness to fill his parents in on what had happened. "Young people are really into politics here," he told them. "Even kids my age!"

Trey's enthusiasm didn't fade. As the year went on, the radical politician lost the election, and the weather grew warmer, he found himself spending more and more time sitting at sidewalk cafés with his classmates, discussing world events and systems of government with kids who'd grown up everywhere from Geneva to Japan.

By the time Trey headed home to Laguna Beach he had learned much more than a new language. The French might have their flaws, but they were passionate about their country. The young people there didn't feel discouraged or powerless in a world controlled by adults. They knew how to take a negative political situation and turn it into something hopeful and positive for the future. *Their* future. Young people really could make a difference. The idea blew him away.

# TREY

## Taking a Stand

Sometimes Trey felt as if he had never left Laguna. The beach was just like he remembered. Stephen and Dieter and his other buds were just like he remembered them, though maybe a little taller. And his house was just like he remembered it—the same old home base, though he spent a lot more nights than he used to sneaking out the side door and hoping he wouldn't find it locked when he got back in the wee hours.

Laguna Beach High School, on the other hand, was a big change from his international school in Paris. He was slowly adjusting to the rhythm of life there, the pace of the classes, the homework assignments. The best part was that, unlike in France, where everyone else scored higher on tests than he did, here Trey was in the top classes.

All in all not too bad a setup, he thought as he slid into a seat in one of his honors classes. Today, his teacher had an announcement to make. An announcement that shook Trey up more than anything else about readjusting to life in Laguna.

"I know there's a protest going on tomorrow against the war in Iraq," the teacher said. "And I know some of you students are planning to miss my class so you can participate in it."

Trey was one of those students.

"Going to a protest is not a legitimate excuse for skipping school," the teacher continued. "I will be assigning an in-class essay tomorrow. There will be no way to make up the points if you miss it."

A student's overall grade in the class was based on his or her points, and when Trey heard the number of points the teacher had assigned to tomorrow's essay, he knew it could make or break a kid's final grade. That was the teacher's goal. If he got a zero for the essay, there would be slim chance he could pull an A for a final grade, despite the fact that he'd done well in class all year.

He couldn't believe it. This attitude was the exact opposite of his teachers' in Paris. There, politics were supposed to play an important role in your life, even if you were a high school kid. Nobody scolded you for missing a few hours of school to take part in a rally. They applauded it. After all, you had to take a stand on important issues. Didn't you?

Trey watched dumbfounded as the teacher turned casually to the blackboard to begin the day's lesson. No one in class seemed phased by the announcement. No one but him. He glanced around and wondered what the other students would elect to do—fight for their beliefs or fight for their B average?

Trey's choice was already made. The way he saw it, some things were more important than grades. He knew that in time he would probably forget the answer to whatever the essay question asked. He would probably even forget his honors class teacher's name and whether he'd had the class second period or third. But he would remember the Iraq War. You had to grow up sometime. You had to take a stand for something so you didn't fall for anything.

# TREY

*Welcome to PAG*

Something had been bothering Trey ever since the Iraq War protest. It wasn't the fact that protesting had meant missing an important in-class assignment that cost him an A in an honors class. He could deal with dropping a grade. Something bigger than that was weighing on his mind.

High school students in Laguna Beach cared about parties. They cared about popularity. A lot of them cared about grades, and about getting into the right college. But nobody seemed to care about politics. Half the time he suspected he was the only one among his friends who bothered to read the newspapers or had a clue what was going on in the world outside the Bubble. But what if the majority of his peers just hadn't been exposed to politics in a positive way?

If anyone was going to change things, why not him? Why not now? So at the beginning of his junior year Trey came up with a game plan.

He approached the administration for permission to form the People's Awareness Group. To his delight, school administrators gave him the go-ahead to set up PAG as an official school club, which students could join and attend during a designated study hour every Thursday.

PAG would function as a kind of study group, overseen by Trey and his friends Jonathan and Polster. The three of them would find issues to discuss, research them thoroughly online, then present the facts and opposing views about the issues in

an unbiased way. They would encourage the class to discuss each issue in—and here was the key—an open, friendly, nonhostile environment. No judgments. No putting down other people's opinions or ideas because they clashed with yours. There was no right or wrong in PAG. Just different points of view.

Trey suffered a few moments of self-doubt before the group got under way. What if nobody signed up? What if everyone just sat there and stared at him? Stephen and Dieter had sometimes done that when he'd mentioned politics years earlier.

He needn't have worried. The class filled up in no time, and Trey was amped on how eager his peers were to learn about issues and then to chime in with their opinions once they understood the facts. Over the year the group conducted lively discussions about everything from euthanasia to abortion, from the presidential election to the separation of church and state.

Sure, there were times when tempers flared in PAG. Trey, Jonathan, or Polster would have to jump in and tell people to chill. But that was cool. At least they cared enough to get worked up about things.

Inspired by the success of PAG, Trey felt ready to take his group to the next level. He wanted to create a group that would inspire and energize young people to live a politically active lifestyle, and help them channel their enthusiasm and potential in positive ways. So he formed Active Young America.

Like PAG, AYA was 100 percent nonjudgmental. Trey wasn't interested in telling anybody what to believe or how to live. What he *did* want to do was to help young people like himself learn how to get involved in their local communities in order to make changes for the better. Sometimes AYA brought in speakers from off campus to talk about issues going on in Orange County. Other times the group organized open-mike nights to showcase young talent.

Trey knew there must be teenagers all over America who were already doing the same sorts of things, but nobody was keeping track of it all or getting the word out. So another goal of AYA would be to document ways that young people were leading productive lives, helping others, and affecting the world around them for the better.

Of course, it wasn't enough to nurture a politically active lifestyle in other teenagers. You had to live it. You had to lead by example. And that's what Trey tried to do.

Sometimes he thought back to sophomore year in Paris and to that memorable day when one of his teachers had demanded to know why he was sitting in class when he should be at a political rally. It was amazing how much one day could change your life. If that teacher could see him now, what would she say? Trey suspected she'd give him an A for effort.

# Morgan

## *At Home in Laguna*

Morgan's parents had been talking about moving to Laguna Beach for so long that she had stopped taking them seriously. She knew they had grown up there and loved it. Even her grandparents were from Laguna Beach. But she figured it was just one of those things. You dream about it, but you don't actually do it.

So when they came home from house hunting in the middle of Morgan's junior year and announced to their five children that they had found a place, Morgan rolled her eyes. "Yeah, sure. Whatever," she said.

When they piled the kids into the car for the fifteen-minute drive from their home in Newport Harbor to the new house—*their* new house—for the first time, Morgan was still in denial. Her parents took her to the beach, drove her to the local high school, and tried to point out all the fun things there were to do in the new town.

"We're not moving to Laguna," Morgan insisted.

"You'll like it here," they assured her.

Were they crazy? It was two weeks before Christmas. She was getting ready to take the SATs, thinking about college. She had a set group of friends she had known since kindergarten, a set schedule at school, a set life. How could they uproot her now?

Morgan kept telling herself the move wasn't going to happen even as cardboard boxes filled up all around her house. Two weeks later, at the beginning of winter break, everything her family owned was packed and she was saying good-bye to all her friends. It seemed like a bad dream. She kept waiting to wake up.

When she realized that wasn't going to happen, she started driving down to Newport Harbor every morning.

"You can't keep doing this," her mother warned her.

"Why not?" Morgan asked. "All my friends are there. I don't know anybody here."

"Just give it a chance," her mother begged. "You'll like it here."

Easy for her to say.

A few days later a boy named Gary, who lived down the street and went to Morgan's new church, knocked on the door and offered to show her around the neighborhood and introduce her to some other kids their age. Morgan reluctantly said okay. She'd go with him, but she wasn't going to be her usual upbeat, outgoing self. She didn't want to be here anyway. Gary ignored her sullen mood and kept up a stream of cheerful conversation.

"Look, there's Christina," he said, spotting a girl in a volleyball uniform walking down the street. He pulled his car over to the curb and rolled down the window. "She's a junior, too. I'll introduce you."

Christina leaned in the window and gave Morgan a friendly greeting, which lightened her mood a little. Christina lived just ten doors down from Morgan and she seemed supernice.

That night at home in her new room, Morgan thought about how much of an effort everyone seemed to be making to help her be happy in Laguna. Everyone except her. Maybe she had been looking at this all wrong. Her old friends were only fifteen minutes away. It wasn't like she was losing them. Maybe she could just double her number of friends—old ones from Newport and new ones from Laguna. It would be easy if all the kids were as welcoming as Gary and Christina.

On her first day of school, Morgan walked into class and stood hesitantly at the front of the room, unsure where to sit. A pretty blonde girl waved her hand and motioned for her to take the empty seat behind hers.

"Hi, I'm Lo," she said when Morgan sat down. They chatted after class and Lo invited her to go to lunch that day. Soon they were eating lunch together every day and Lo was introducing her to lots of new people. She invited Morgan out for sushi with a bunch of girls, and took her to her very first Laguna party with lots of senior guys. *Cute* senior guys. Morgan had overlooked one of the major advantages of switching to a new school. New boys.

As she settled into life in Laguna Beach, Morgan found herself making the drive back to Newport Harbor less often, though she still kept in touch with her old friends. Sometimes one of them would give her a pitying look and ask, "Don't you miss home?"

Morgan would have to stop and think. Home? What were they talking about? Laguna Beach was home now. She hated to admit it, but her mom and dad were right. She *did* like it here.

# MORGAN
## Four Going on Twenty-four

"Two tuna sandwiches, please."

Five-year-old Morgan glanced around Mother's Market while her mom gave their order, paid, and waited for the girl at the counter to count back her change. The Newport Beach lunch spot was one of their favorites and Morgan was looking forward to hanging out with her mom, having a sandwich, and enjoying the sun-drenched summer afternoon. But back in the car she got an unappetizing surprise. She peeled back the wrapper to find that juice from a dill pickle had leaked all over. Everything was soaked—the wrapper, the bread, even the tuna.

"Mom, this sandwich is gross," Morgan said. "It's all soggy. I didn't even want a pickle."

"You can have mine," her mom offered.

"No, that's okay." Morgan wrinkled her nose at the sand-

wich. Reluctantly she took a bite. Just as she suspected. Totally gross.

Before her mom could stop her, Morgan rewrapped the sandwich, got out of the car, and marched back into Mother's. Though her head barely reached the top of the counter, she managed to get the countergirl's attention and explain the problem.

"I'm not going to give you a new sandwich," the girl said, shaking her head. "I can't do that."

Morgan knew she was a five-year-old taking on a grown-up—and by now drawing the attention of every other grown-up nearby—but so what? It wasn't fair. Why should they be able to treat her like that just because she was a kid?

"I want to speak to the manager!" she demanded in her high-pitched, little-girl voice.

The countergirl shrugged, then went off in search of the manager. Morgan waited patiently, then politely explained the situation when the manager arrived.

To the surprise of the countergirl but not Morgan's mom (she already knew her daughter wasn't afraid to stand up to any-one), when Morgan strolled casually back out into the bright af-ternoon sun, she was clutching a fresh, unsoggy tuna sandwich.

# MORGAN
## Junior Lifeguards

Morgan gazed contentedly out the window at the expanse of blue sky and the frothy waves lapping the shore below it. She loved going to elementary school on the beach. While other kids were stuck in stuffy gymnasiums, her class got to have PE in the fresh air on the sand. While other kids had to ride a yellow bus to school, she and her friends rode their bikes along the boardwalk, enjoying the cool ocean breezes. In the afternoons on the way home to Lido Island, where they lived, they would stop for shaved ices while they plotted out their next adventure. One of their favorites was jumping off the twenty-foot island bridge into the bay, school clothes and all.

The beach found its way into almost every aspect of Morgan's life, from waking up in the morning and seeing a view of the bay out her bedroom window to logging so many hours in her family's backyard pool that her father referred to her as a "little fish."

Like many of the kids who grew up alongside the Southern California coast, Morgan took part in Junior Lifeguards, a summer program that taught everything from ocean safety to CPR to bodyboarding. The highlight of the camp was always the one-mile swim and running race. Morgan looked forward to it all year.

When she was ten, she woke up on the morning of Junior Lifeguards race day with a sense of breathless anticipation. The day was bright and clear, but with bracing winds.

When she and her family got to the beach, she realized just how strong those winds really were. Enormous waves were crashing onto the sand. The red flag had been put up, the warning sign for dangerous waters, and it was whipping around wildly. Would they call the swim off? She hoped not.

Morgan took her place with the other runners and, at the starting signal, tore off as fast as she could along the beach. As she neared the mark to start the one-mile swim, she saw to her dismay that lifeguards were attempting to keep the junior contestants out of the water. Some of the kids were heeding their advice and slowing down or stopping to catch their breath. But Morgan had waited all year for this. She wasn't going to let a little wind stop her.

Ignoring them, she charged into the ocean. The next thing she knew, the waves were pounding and tossing her like crazy. The roar of the surf drowned out the lifeguards' yells as she gasped for air, struggled through the waves, and ultimately crossed the finish line with a huge smile on her face.

A few of the lifeguards shook their heads when they saw her dripping wet and exhausted. She shrugged apologetically and smiled. They just didn't understand. Nothing got between Morgan and the beach.

# Lo

## *The Scariest Halloween Ever*

Everyone in Laguna Beach knew the rule when it came to parties: Being a guest was great, being a host was the worst. Mention the word "party," and before you know it, the entire teenage population of Laguna Beach gets wind of it and shows up on your doorstep.

Still, Lo had never had a party. It was junior year. There wasn't that much time left. "Why not?" she figured. Her mom and dad were out of town, it was Halloween weekend, and there was nothing else going on.

"I'll just tell my good friends," she assured herself. "I'll keep it small."

Hearing about her plans, her younger brother quickly made his own: to spend the night at a neighbor's house in Three Arch, the gated community where they lived, and get out of the way.

Getting ready for the party that evening, Lo and her friends could feel their excitement mounting. Who would show up? Who would hook up? Would anyone bring any new cute guys?

It seemed like one minute they were all doing their makeup and waiting for their friends to arrive and the next, the house was full of music, laughter, and . . . *people.* People were dancing in the living room. People were spilling out the front door into the yard. A lot of them were barely recognizable in their costumes. Lo glanced across the kitchen and spotted a group of guys she'd never seen before. She tapped a friend on the shoulder. "Who are they?" she asked. "Do you know them?" Nobody had any idea who they were.

This was getting totally out of control. Lo walked out the front door to get some air and saw cars parked everywhere. What were the neighbors going to say? What were her parents going to say if they found out? What if the house got trashed?! She felt herself alternating between panic and anger.

She marched back in the kitchen and scrambled onto the kitchen table. "Who are you??!" she shouted to the crowd. "Get out of my house!"

Nobody paid any attention. They were having too much fun. Just like I would be, thought Lo, if this party was in somebody else's house.

It was 3:00 A.M. by the time the last partygoers trickled out into the night. Lo glanced around, unsure where to start the massive clean-up project ahead. The next morning she was still wearily lugging bags of trash out and struggling to get the countless dirty footprints off her family's polished hardwood floors.

Fortunately, the weekly housekeeper showed up at midmorning. Lo felt so guilty that she not only handed over a generous tip, but came clean to her parents about the festivities when they got home.

"Don't worry," she assured them. "I learned my lesson. I won't be having any more parties here."

Laguna Beach High School lore was right: It was much, much better to go to a party than to give one.

# CHRISTINA

## A Dozen Roses

"Christina," the teacher called. "I'd like a word with you, please."

Was she in trouble? Christina couldn't think of anything she had done wrong in English class, but it looked like she was about to get sent to the principal's office. Instead, the teacher told her to go to the library.

"I need you to pick up a copy of this book for me," she explained, giving her a note with a title and author printed on it. It was a strange request, but Christina took the note and headed off to the school library.

When she got there, the librarian read the slip of paper and nodded. Instead of giving her a book, she handed Christina a rose.

"What's this for?" Christina asked.

"Read the note," said the librarian. Attached to the rose was a piece of paper with the first line of a poem and instructions to see another teacher.

"I don't understand," said Christina. "Is this a joke?"

The librarian shrugged. "I suppose you'd better go and find out."

Christina walked down the hall to the classroom of the next teacher whose name was on the note. She, too, handed Christina a rose and a letter inscribed with the second line of the poem. Below it was a message to go to yet another classroom.

And so it went until Christina had collected a dozen roses in different colors from a dozen different teachers along with a dozen notes. Together the lines on the notes made up a complete poem. Under the poem's last line was a message instructing her to go back to her original classroom.

Who could be behind this? Did someone have a secret crush on her? If so, this was not a very secret way of letting her know.

Christina walked back into English, her arms full of roses. Sitting on top of the teacher's desk was a chocolate cake with white icing and the word PROM? written across it in purple.

It was the most elaborate, romantic invitation Christina had ever gotten, but she still had no idea who was behind it. By now there were only a few minutes left before the bell rang, so the class split the cake and helped Christina speculate on who the mystery man might be. The teacher insisted that she had no idea.

At the end of the school day, she still didn't have a clue. She was dying to know who had gone through all this trouble to ask her to her junior prom. How much longer was she going to be kept in suspense?

She got the answer when she saw her car in the school parking lot. Across the windshield was taped an enormous sign that read "Will you go to prom with me?" Underneath it was the name of her friend Trey C., from her English class.

English class? Christina realized her secret admirer had been sitting right there the whole time, eating cake and playing along with the guessing game, enjoying her reaction.

Just then he walked up. "So?" he asked, smiling. "What's your answer?"

"Of course I'll go with you," she said, giving him a hug. "But I can't believe you sent me all over the school when you were sitting right there. You could have just asked me, you know."

"True," he said. "I could have. But it was more fun this way."

# CHRISTINA
## Toilet Paper Terrors

Christina and her friends from the neighborhood liked playing ball, splashing in her parents' pool, bouncing on the trampoline in her backyard, and all the usual kid stuff. But their favorite game of all was toilet papering.

By fifth grade they were masters of the sneak attack, creeping up to neighbors' houses under the cover of night to lob dozens of fat, white tissue rolls into treetops, over roofs, and onto eves. They would watch with glee as the ends unwound

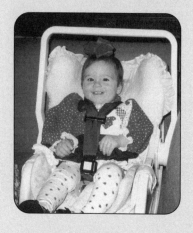

and rippled like graceful kite tails over every branch and gutter. By the time they had finished with a place it usually looked like a giant gingerbread house decked in messy white icing.

Christina's friends sometimes laughed about the fact that she, a preacher's kid, was such a willing accomplice. "Isn't toilet papering a sin or something?" they'd tease. Then Christina would patiently explain for the thousandth time that just because she went to church every Sunday it didn't mean she was a Bible freak or a goody-goody. She was normal. She enjoyed toilet papering as much as the next kid.

Besides, "Smokin' Schuller" (as Christina's dad called her) was the pitcher for her softball team and a member of the girls' All-Stars. She had the best throwing arm of any of them. That made her the toilet-papering gang's secret weapon when it came to hitting the most important spots on their targets.

One evening Christina slipped out of her house just after twilight, telling her parents she was going to a friend's. Instead, she and two of the other girls from her neighborhood went on a TP rampage, sneaking from house to house clutching bags of toilet paper rolls that they had carefully secreted out of their houses and stashed away ahead of time.

They had worked their way down the block, giggling hysterically at the results of their handiwork, and were now on their fourth house. Christina had her arm drawn back, poised to heave a fresh roll of toilet paper skyward, when she first heard the noise.

"What was that?" she whispered nervously to one of her friends. "Did you hear something?"

"I didn't hear anything—"

"Sshhhh!" Christina shushed her and listened again. She was sure she heard a snuffling noise somewhere nearby. "There it is again! I think there might be a dog around here."

A low, menacing growl sounded from close behind them. As if in slow motion, all three girls turned to stare in the direction of whatever had made the noise.

*Wooooooooffffff!!!!*

The next thing Christina knew, an enormous dog came bounding out of the backyard and charged toward them, teeth bared, barking loudly enough to wake up everyone on the block.

"Aaaaaaaahhhhhggggghh!" the girls screamed. Abandoned rolls of toilet paper bounced and skittered over the lawn as they flung their bags away and tore out of the yard, the dog barking ferociously at their heels.

Christina flew toward home. She knew this was the fastest she had run in her life, faster than she had ever raced around the bases in softball. She was almost sure she could feel the dog's hot breath on the back of her legs and hear it gnashing its pointed teeth. Any second now she expected its enormous jaws to latch onto her ankle and start ripping her to pieces.

"Please God," she panted as she ran. "Don't let the dog kill me! I swear, I'll never do it again!"

At last she reached the safety of her house and slammed the door behind her. "Thank you, thank you, thank you," she mouthed in a silent prayer, wiping the sweat off her forehead with one trembling hand. Boy, she thought. That was a close one.

Twenty minutes later she had made a full recovery. She told her parents she was going to a friend's, but instead she sneaked down the block and toilet papered the next house in line.

At least if anyone asked her at church that Sunday whether she had prayed this week, Christina could honestly say yes, she had. She hoped God would let her slide just this once. She figured He probably would if He had any idea how much fun toilet papering can be when you're ten years old.

# CHRISTINA
## Music Woman

"Mom, I'm going to audition for *The Music Man,*" Christina announced as she walked into the kitchen one day after school. Volleyball season had just ended, and this was her senior year—her last chance to perform in the annual school musical.

She had always loved to sing. She sang in church choirs, in the shower, in the car, everywhere. She had been doing it since her toddler days, when she belted out Disney tunes in the bathtub. But since starting freshman year volleyball had kept her too busy to try out for school productions. She had either been in playoffs or felt too exhausted to think about tackling another big project when the season wound down. Until now. Christina knew it was this year or never.

Her mother wanted to be supportive, but she didn't want Christina to get her hopes up. "Drama is very competitive at your school," she warned. "Some of these kids have been acting for years."

"I just thought it would be fun to try out," Christina assured her. "I won't be disappointed if I don't get cast."

As her mother had predicted, during the first day of tryouts Christina was clumped into a group of students who were unknown to the drama regulars and—Christina assumed—unlikely to get parts.

To her mom's amazement, Christina made cut after cut, announcing each one when she came home from school. "Well, I'm still in there. They haven't gotten rid of me yet!" It was starting to look promising. She might land a small role after all.

Then one day, Christina walked in and stood there speechless. Oh no, thought her mother. Was that disappointment on her daughter's face? Shock? What should she say to console her?

"Guess what? I got the lead!" Christina burst out. "I'm going to play Marian the Librarian in *The Music Man!*"

# TREY

Trey put the finishing touches on the hat, then stood back and admired it. It had started as a plain navy blue trucker cap. Then Trey had sewn sections of yellow, blue, and gray polka dot material from Goodwill to it. Next he'd attached a section of black handkerchief to one side. Then he'd added buttons and shoelaces and a few random bits of old clothing.

For several months now, he and a buddy who shared his interest in design had been hanging out at his house after school, having fun redesigning shirts and adding their own embellishments to hats. First they'd stocked up on needles and thread. Then they'd collected material by rummaging through bins at the local Goodwill store or salvaging it from a local clothing factory's discards.

But so far this was the first hat Trey considered truly finished. He was really proud of it. Should he wear it to school? What if people laughed? He debated, then decided to go for it.

"Dude, that's a cool hat," someone said almost as soon as he walked into class the next morning.

"Hey, great hat. Where'd you get it?" The compliments continued all day. People couldn't believe Trey had made the hat himself.

"Can you make one for me?" they all wanted to know.

"Sure," Trey said, happy people actually liked his work.

He went home and started making more hats. He got ideas for designs in the most random ways. He might see a painting or a photo. Or he might simply be lying down on the beach and see a layer of sand below a layer of water below a layer of sky. He'd take that image and work it into a pattern with stripes of color based on the way the beach had looked. Later, whenever he looked at the finished product, he'd remember the image that had inspired it. Other times a box of old buttons or something else Trey found lying around his house would spark his imagination and he'd work them into what he was sewing.

The problem was that he worked really hard on every hat. Each one was unique. He hated to give them away. He kept making excuses to people at school when they asked, "Where's that hat you promised me?"

Dieter finally solved the problem. One afternoon while he was hanging out at Trey's house, he spied a great hat. He just sort of decided to take it along that evening when he went home. Trey had promised him one months ago anyway.

"Hey," Trey protested as Dieter headed out the door. "I made that hat for my dad for Father's Day."

Dieter shrugged and put the hat on his head. "Just give your dad another one," he said. "I know you'll make more."

# TREY
## Animal Instincts

By the time Trey and his parents set off on safari in South Africa, the 14-year-old was already an experienced traveler. He'd been to Mexico, Costa Rica, and most recently to visit his brother Trevor in Tanzania, where Trey had barely survived a vicious dodgeball match at the all-girls' school where Trevor taught.

The first few days of the trek proved as incredible as Trey had hoped. He loved seeing the animals up close in their natural habitat, the scenery and the food were exotic, and the rustic campsites made you feel like you were sleeping in the heart of nature's last truly untamed kingdom, side by side with all kinds of wildlife. Every night safari staff armed with guns escorted the travelers back to their tents, waited until they zipped themselves in, and made sure they were equipped with a horn and a whistle—*just in case.*

"Just in case of what?" Trey asked.

"In case an animal sneaks out of the bushes," he was told.

"Don't worry," his parents assured him. "The staff says we're completely safe."

"Completely safe," the staff agreed.

Like his parents, Trey was always amped for new adventures when it came to travel. He didn't need a five-star hotel with mints on the pillow to enjoy the trip. Still, he couldn't help wishing he had a gun next to his pillow instead of a horn and a whistle. He wouldn't want to run into some of that African wildlife under cover of night armed with only a whistle. He always double-checked to make sure the zipper of his tent was fully closed.

A few nights into the trip, he was lying in bed replaying the day's highlights in his mind when he heard a strange sound. *Rat-*

*a-tat-tat. Thump, thump, thump. Rat-a-tat-tat. Thump, thump, thump.* Something huge was pacing back and forth in front of his tent. Trey swallowed hard and tried not to panic. His parents were just a few feet away, asleep in the next tent.

"Mom?" Trey called, a slight quiver in his voice.

"Yes?"

"There's a carnivore outside my tent!"

"It's okay, Trey," she called back calmly. "It'll go away. Just go back to sleep."

Go to sleep! Was she crazy?! There was no way he could sleep. The hours dragged by as Trey lay awake listening to whatever was outside making its patient trek back and forth. *Rat-a-tat-tat. Thump, thump, thump.*

At some point he finally drifted off, lulled in spite of himself by the rhythmic sound. He awoke in the morning, grateful to see the sunlight streaming in through the canvas of his tent and to hear the sounds of other travelers moving around the campsite. Maybe the mysterious nocturnal noises had been nothing more than a figment of his imagination.

He unzipped the closure and scrambled out. There, in front of the tent, just a few feet from where he'd been sleeping, was a huge flattened swath of grass.

"It was a lion!" Trey shouted. "Mom, look at this! I knew it was a lion!"

His mom strolled over and inspected the patch of grass.

"Hmmm," she said casually. "That was close, wasn't it?"

# LAUREN AND STEPHEN

## Chick Magnet

Who cared if Cache was only a junior when Lauren was starting her senior year? The guy was hot. Lauren's crush on the adorable surfer with the beat-up white VW bug and the shaggy blond hair was such a well-known fact among her friends that they'd taken to crying out "C-a-a-a-che money!" to tease her.

"I love Cache," she'd reply good-naturedly. "He's so cute. I'm gonna marry him!"

So it was a shock to Lauren when Cache's friend broke the bad news. "Oh, man," he told her. "Sorry, but Cache already has a girlfriend."

"Oh," was all Lauren could think to say. Secretly, her heart sank. Senior year hadn't been going too well, romantically speaking, and now she had just gotten denied by a younger guy. "I'm just done," she told herself. "I am never gonna date anyone."

Later that day she was still bummed out. Since business was slow at the surf shop where she worked and the owners were superlaidback, Lauren wandered two shops down, as she often did, to chat with Stephen and keep him company at his job. Seeing him always cheered her up.

Lauren filled Stephen in on the latest developments with Cache, concluding her story with "There is no one to date in our school!"

"I'll find you someone," he assured her.

"Yeah, right," she said hopelessly.

Stephen abruptly changed the subject. "Hey, do you still have any of your old Barbie dolls?"

"What?"

"Old Barbies. I'm going as a chick magnet for Halloween tomorrow night and I want to sew Barbies to my shirt."

"Whose party are you going to?" Lauren knew the answer before she asked the question.

"Kristin's," he mumbled, looking away. Stephen knew Lauren had never been exactly thrilled about the idea of him dating Kristin. It seemed like the two girls had disliked each other from the second they laid eyes on each other.

Lauren sighed. Lately she'd been putting in a lot of hours listening to her closest guy friend agonize over his relationship problems. In her opinion, Kristin just wasn't worth it. She resisted the urge to tell him to just end it with the girl already.

"Sure," she said. "My mom probably has my old Barbie dolls packed away somewhere in the house. Come over tomorrow."

"Great! Thanks," said Stephen. "And don't worry. We'll find someone for you to go out with."

The next night when Stephen showed up, Lauren had the Barbie dolls ready. She even sewed them to his shirt, while he hung out in her room thumbing through her yearbook.

"Hey," he said, jabbing his finger at a picture. "How about this guy? You could date him."

Lauren glanced up from her sewing. "No way!"

He flipped through a few more pages. "Him!" Stephen exclaimed. "He's a great guy. I had geometry with him, I think."

Lauren shook her head.

And so it went. On and on, with Stephen suggesting practically every guy in their class and then all the underclassmen, and Lauren coming up with one reason or another why they were all undateable.

At last Stephen began to get an inkling that maybe Lauren was trying to tell him something. Was she rejecting all the other guys because she secretly wanted to date him? Should he make a move? Would it be weird? They'd been friends forever, but he'd always thought Lauren was cute. He leaned over and kissed her.

After a few minutes of kissing Lauren, Stephen wasn't even sure he wanted to go to Kristin's party anymore, but he was starting to get confused. Better to get out of there and get his head cleared.

"I should get going," he said. "Thanks for the Barbies."

"Sure," said Lauren, walking him out.

At the front door, Stephen stopped and turned around to kiss Lauren good-bye.

"See?" he said. "I told you we'd find someone."

Later that night Stephen couldn't keep his mind on the party. Finally, he snuck away, closed himself in an empty room, and pulled out his cell phone.

"Lauren? Hey, it's me. What are you doing?"

Lauren was at a different party, but she wasn't having much fun, either. So she offered to slip out long enough to help Stephen make a getaway. "You're my driver," she told Lo as she grabbed her friend's sleeve and steered her toward the car. "We're kidnapping Stephen."

Stephen was waiting. As the car slowed down in front of Kristin's house, he bolted out the door. Lo floored it and they headed back to the other party.

No sooner had they walked in the door than Lauren spied, of all people, Cache. Stephen and Lo wandered off to talk to some of their friends and Lauren slipped into the seat next to her crush.

It was the first time they'd said much more than "hello" to each other. Maybe it was the recent turn of events with Stephen or maybe the Halloween costume, but for some reason Lauren felt bolder. Before she knew what she was doing, she asked Cache point blank whether the story she'd heard was true.

"I don't have a girlfriend," he said. "Who told you I did?"

The next thing she knew, she and Cache were kissing.

*Right in front of Stephen.* Lauren saw him standing there, across the room, staring at her. He looked like she'd smacked him across the face. Lauren was furious with herself. What the hell was she doing?

She made up an excuse to get away from Cache and ran off in search of Lo. "Can we please get out of here," she begged.

"Sure." Lo shrugged. "If you want to."

She and Lauren headed for the door. Stephen followed sullenly.

Later, on the way home, Lo slipped a CD she'd made into the deck in an effort to liven up the mood. Why did everybody seem so depressed tonight?

"Hey, Stephen," she called over the music filling the car. "Do you like my chick mix?"

Stephen, still in his Barbie-covered shirt, scowled from the backseat.

"Chicks suck," he muttered, glaring out the window.

# Stephen and Dieter

## Caught in the Middle

*Brrrrinnnng!*

"What's up?" Dieter answered his cell phone, annoyed that someone was calling him in the middle of the hockey game.

"Hey, Dieter. It's Kristin. Listen, I have to ask you something about Stephen."

"Um . . . okay," said Dieter hesitantly, glancing over at Stephen who was sitting right next to him, watching the players race up and down the ice with the puck.

Dieter listened to Kristin's question then tried to answer it as diplomatically as he could. She thanked him and hung up.

No sooner had Dieter turned his attention back to the game than his phone rang again.

"Hi, Dieter. It's Lauren. I have to ask you something about Stephen."

Dieter sighed resignedly and resisted the urge to punch his friend.

"Okay," he said. "What's the question?"

He hated being stuck in the middle like this. If Stephen was going to hook up with two girls at once, he didn't want to be a part of the drama that was bound to follow when one or the other found out. He liked both Lauren and Kristin a lot, and he didn't want to see either of them get hurt.

But Stephen was his bro. If he was on anyone's side, it had to be Stephen's. They always stood by each other, even years earlier when standing by each other usually meant standing side by side on the yellow line as a punishment for breaking the rules in recess.

In fact, the only fights Stephen and Dieter ever had erupted

when one gave the other advice about girls. The advice was always well-meaning—and usually good—but that didn't make the other guy want to hear it. The way Dieter saw things, he and Stephen were bros for life. If Stephen wanted to put himself in some romantic Bermuda triangle, Dieter wasn't going to risk their friendship by pointing out the dangers.

Dieter slipped the cell phone back into his pocket and congratulated himself on having skated through what could have been a minefield.

But then the phone rang again. And again. The girls kept coming up with more questions. Sharp, tricky questions that made him wonder if maybe they suspected he wasn't quite being honest with them. Dieter did his best, but he was starting to get confused about what he had said to whom.

"Hang on, Lauren . . . sorry! I mean Kristin." He put a hand over the phone to buy himself a few seconds. He needed to clear his head. He would have asked Stephen a quick, whispered question to help him get his stories straight, but it was now between periods, and Stephen had wandered off to get something to eat at the concession stand.

Dieter took a deep breath. Then he gave it a shot.

"WHAT?!" the voice on the other end exploded. "That's just the opposite of what you told me a few minutes ago!"

Shit! thought Dieter. They were in for it now.

He knew he would probably catch hell for lying to the girls. After all, they were his friends, too. He should have been completely honest with them. And he would have if he could have—if only it hadn't meant betraying Stephen. Dieter could never do that.

A bro is a bro. You stand by him no matter what.

# JESSICA AND ALEX H.

## Fair Game

Jessica's mom couldn't have put it more plainly: You can't have the guy unless you get the grades.

So what if her marks in school had slipped since she started dating Mike three months ago? What was the big deal? Jessica had never really struggled academically. Even back in kindergarten she was so far ahead of everyone that she ended up in a reading group for first graders. Besides, she was just a sophomore. It wasn't like she had to worry about getting into college yet. And she was smitten with Mike. He was gorgeous *and* he was a senior. She couldn't believe he was even interested in her. In the big picture, wasn't having your first real boyfriend infinitely more important than keeping up with homework every day?

So, why was her mom being so unreasonable? After her last report card, Jessica had been banned from talking on the phone with Mike. Her mom had taken away her cell, forbidden her to use the house phone for social calls, and locked up her computer, which meant no e-mail.

Jessica couldn't even bitch to her girlfriends like Alex H. about the misery of life at home these days because they didn't eat lunch together (that was practically the only time she got to see Mike anymore) and putting it in a note was too risky, as Jessica had learned when one of her teachers snatched a note she was passing to Alex right out of her hands and read it aloud. She would have died before she let the whole class know that her mother was now threatening not to let her go out with Mike at all until her grades improved.

"You can't just take *everything* away from me!" Jessica argued, but it was no use. She did her best to find ways around her mom's rules, but Mike was getting fed up with having a girlfriend he couldn't see for more than an hour a day.

Jessica had a bad feeling about going to lunch with her boyfriend that afternoon. She could tell by the way the conversation kept stalling and how Mike kept avoiding her gaze that he wanted to say something, but didn't know how. Instinct told her that whatever it was, she wasn't going to be happy to hear it. Maybe he was going to suggest they take a break for a few weeks until she got her mom under control.

It was worse than she'd feared. Right in the middle of lunch he broke up with her. She lost her appetite indefinitely.

Still in shock, Jessica went back to school and sat down in her usual seat in English class, staring numbly at the blackboard. Alex cast a worried glance in her direction, then looked over at Talan, who was sitting next to Jessica.

"Is she okay?" Talan asked Alex, giving Jessica a puzzled look.

"I'm fine," Jessica replied in a monotone. She was determined to act like nothing was wrong, even though she was about to burst into tears any minute. She tried to muster a reassuring smile for Talan, but seeing the concern on his face was too much. She started sobbing so hard she almost hyperventilated. Alex and Talan rushed her out into the hallway and tried to calm her down. She wasn't sure how she managed to get through the rest of the day, but somehow she did. She felt so grateful to both of them. It was a good thing she had such amazing, sympathetic, supportive friends to lean on.

Four days later, Jessica was still moping through the halls, half afraid of running into Mike, half hoping to. What would he do when they saw each other? Ignore her? Act casual? Pull her aside apologetically and beg her to go out with him again?

Whatever she was expecting, it wasn't what she saw. There was Mike, strolling happily down the hall hand in hand with . . . Alex, Jessica's supposed close friend.

It was all Jessica could do not to start hyperventilating all over again. She stared at them as they passed. Neither one of them even seemed to notice she was standing there. She was devastated.

Not only had she lost a boyfriend, she had lost a girlfriend. (The two of them would barely speak again until two years later, when Mike dumped Alex as heartlessly as he had dumped Jessica, and Jessica felt too bad for her to stay mad any longer.)

She couldn't be sure yet, but Jessica's guess was that she would probably lose some other friends over this, too. Girls who had known Alex longer and better than they knew her might take Alex's side. Others would probably tell her to just get over it. Move on. How hard can you fall for a guy in three months?

A few weeks later Jessica saw a new girl she recognized from school sitting in Gina's pizza parlor. She decided to go over and say hello before any of her former friends could badmouth her. She wasn't sure they would, but she didn't want to take a chance.

"Hi," she said. "I'm Jessica. I just wanted to introduce myself before you hear anything about me from other people."

"Nice to meet you," said the girl. "I'm Kristin."

# JESSICA AND DIETER

## Talan's Prediction Comes True

Jessica was far from over being dumped by her boyfriend, Mike, and betrayed by her girlfriend, Alex H., who moved in for the kill just four days after Mike broke Jessica's heart. Tonight, to make herself feel better, she was at a party hooking up with a cute junior.

She couldn't believe it when Dieter, another junior who was

hosting the party, flew over in a rage and kicked them out of his house. What was his problem? They were only kissing.

"Just take her home," Dieter ordered.

What a jerk, Jessica thought. Why was he being so mean? "Fine," she told Dieter angrily, gathering up her purse and heading for the door. "Forget it. I'll leave."

She was at a complete loss for words when Dieter called her a few days later and invited her to go to the beach with him. What he said when they got there shocked her even more. He confessed that he'd had a crush on her for a long time, but was dating another girl. He was really sorry for kicking her out, but he couldn't stand to see her hook up with his friend in his own house.

"I'm still getting over someone," Jessica told him cautiously. "I don't want a boyfriend right now."

They continued to walk and talk, eventually ending up at Dieter's friend Joe's house. Talan was already there, hanging out with Joe when they arrived. He watched them talking for a few minutes, then he pulled Dieter aside.

"You two are gonna be together," he predicted.

"No," Dieter said, shaking his head, "She doesn't want a boyfriend."

Talan shrugged. "Wait and see," he said with a smile. "You two are definitely gonna be together."

One week later, Talan's prediction came true. Dieter and Jessica were a couple. Mike would soon be nothing but a memory. Talan always thought he should have put money on that bet he made with Dieter.

# JASON

## *Into the Wilderness*

Jason had been getting in his fair share of trouble, but totaling the BMW was the last straw. Chilling with friends, hanging out at the beach, and going to parties was great, but since the beginning of junior year Jason had been staying out so late so often that he felt exhausted and his grades were slipping. His parents, his teachers, and his coaches were disappointed in him. Worse, he was disappointed in himself.

After the BMW bit the dust, he sat down with his mom and dad and had a long, heart-to-heart talk. They all agreed. It was time to check out of high school, say good-bye to Laguna Beach for a while, and get a change of scenery.

But now, as he gazed out over the rugged Utah terrain,

Jason couldn't help thinking that this was a little *too* drastic a change of scenery. He'd agreed to spend the next weeks roughing it with a group of guys his age, spending his nights camping out and his days on long, grueling trail hikes. But he hadn't counted on the fact that the place would be about a hundred miles from nowhere. Nothing but wilderness as far as the eye could see. He thought longingly about home and the warm, sun-drenched Southern California beaches.

"The first thing you've gotta be able to do," said one of the staff members, abruptly breaking into Jason's train of thought, "is start a fire."

"A fire?" asked Jason.

"Sure. You wanna be able to cook your food, don't you?"

Was he kidding? Jason hoped so, but the guy looked dead serious. There'd be no home-cooked meals here, no restaurants, no snacks, no sushi or Italian. He wondered what they could possibly find to eat in the middle of nowhere.

The Wahlers had never been big on family camping trips, and Jason had no idea how to start a fire from scratch. But he followed instructions, fashioning a bow-and-arrow-shaped device out of sticks and working the pieces together repeatedly until at last the point glowed red and a rewarding puff of smoke appeared.

After passing his trial by fire, he met the other five teenage guys who would be in his group and the staff member who would guide them through the wilderness. Though the place left a lot to be desired eating- and sleeping-wise and he felt cold and tired 24-7, Jason was surprised at how easily he hit it off with everyone. Even more surprising, he discovered that with no TV, no parties, no girls, nothing but the scenery and the stars to contemplate, he had a lot of time on his hands to think. He thought about what he wanted, what he didn't want, and what really mattered. Who cared about a BMW? It was only a car.

After a few more weeks of roughing it, Jason bid good-bye to the Utah wilderness. The ordeal wasn't over—he still had to survive six months of rigid boarding school, with chores and strict classes, before he'd be home again for good—but, so what? He'd get through it. He'd gotten his priorities straight and he knew what mattered. So what if people gossip, like they always do in Laguna Beach? So what if some girl gets mad over something you say or don't say?

Long after he got back home and settled into life in Laguna Beach once more, people would ask Jason what it was like out there in the wild. He always told them it was cool. Better than that, actually. It was one of the best experiences of his life. Most of the time they'd raise a skeptical eyebrow. "Yeah, right," they'd say. "No way." But so what? Let them think what they want. He knew what mattered.

# Jason and Jeff B.

## The 360

Life in Laguna Beach was good for Jeff B. in fifth grade. He was at the top of his class, getting straight As without really trying, girls liked him, and—more important to a ten-year-old guy—he was the best athlete among his friends. He was good at every sport that mattered, from baseball to skateboarding. Especially skateboarding, thanks to the hours he spent riding his board around town and practicing on the half pipe behind his house.

Then this new kid from Laguna Hills named Jason showed up at school. The guy seemed pretty cool, and before long "J-Wahl"—as they nicknamed him—started hanging out with Jeff, Cedric, and the rest of their friends. There was just one problem: Jason was better at everything sports-related than Jeff. Especially skateboarding. I mean, the guy could do a 360 flip. All Jeff could do was a varial flip—definitely not in the same league as a 360. The competition was on.

"That's a pretty gnarly trick," Jeff told Jason one day after school, watching him perform the flip effortlessly.

"Thanks, man," said Jason.

Jeff went home and practiced. And practiced. And practiced some more.

He never did master a 360, but—more important once they had left fifth grade behind them—he and Jason stayed friends long after skateboarding ceased to be the thing that mattered most in life.

# JESSICA ANd DIETER

## Rocky Road

The best part of dating Dieter was that Jessica got to know all the seniors and hang out with them while she was still a junior. The worst part was the jealousy. To everyone outside their relationship, Dieter was the nice guy they had known forever and grown up with. But he had a suspicious, controlling streak that stretched all the way back to his first girlfriend in elementary school, and he hadn't managed to lighten up a whole lot since then. Even he admitted he was the jealous type.

When his ex-girlfriend sat on his lap in the middle of the quad, he knew it didn't mean anything. He wasn't going to cheat on Jessica. He loved her. But he could hardly stand for her to talk to another guy.

Jessica was starting to feel like she spent all her time sitting in the corner at parties while Dieter had fun with his friends. Thank God for Kristin. Since Kristin was dating Stephen and the four of them spent so much time together, Kristin became Jessica's closest confidante.

"If Dieter and I go a day without a fight it's a miracle," Jessica lamented to Kristin. "I don't know what to do."

"You should do whatever *you* want to do," Kristin advised. "If you break up with him, I'll be there for you. Don't worry. You won't be alone."

When Jessica needed a guy's perspective on relationships and romance, she sometimes turned to her friend Jason, who was also a junior. The two of them could talk about anything. Sure, Jessica thought Jason was hot. Who didn't? But she fought the urge to feel jealous when he confided in her about girls he had hooked up with. That's what friends are for, right? You're supposed to be able to tell them anything and have them listen without freaking out or judging you.

Whenever her thoughts drifted to what it would be like to be with Jason, Jessica told herself not to go there. She wouldn't want to risk ruining their friendship. Neither would he. She had

no idea that less than a year later, after Dieter had left for college and their rocky relationship finally ended, Jason would turn out to have a romantic side hidden under his bad-boy exterior. She never dreamed that he would surprise her by taking her to the beach on a moonlit evening, where they would lie on a blanket and watch the stars, and he would ask her to be his girlfriend. That was still months away. For now, Jason was just a good friend. He gave her the same advice as Kristin: "Do whatever *you* want to do."

Jessica figured it must be good advice if she kept hearing it. So she filed it away in the back of her mind. By the time her senior year rolled around, she had made it her motto. She would do what she wanted to do no matter what it was and no matter what anybody else thought.

# Jason and Cedric

## The Brawl

It was supposed to be one of the hottest clubs in Laguna Hills, so Jason, Cedric, and another friend decided they had to check it out. Now that they were juniors, with cars and driver's licenses, they might as well put them to good use and cruise to some new places.

Cedric glanced over at Jason approvingly. He still remembered his first impression of J-Wahl when he had moved to the beach from Laguna Hills years earlier. They'd gotten along from the moment they met, but the guy had dressed like a dork—bad jeans and chains around his neck. "Dude, that look might have worked inland, but not in Laguna Beach," Cedric had told him.

You had to give Jason credit for the way he had cultivated the Laguna Beach style since then. Cedric wondered if the entire crowd inside this Laguna Hills club would look like they had raided Jason's old wardrobe.

The place didn't quite live up to its reputation, but the night had still been fun. Now it was winding down and Cedric was leaning against his car in the parking lot waiting for Jason and their other buddy to show up. He wondered if maybe J-Wahl had hooked up with some girl. Cedric was still getting used to the new and improved Jason. For years he had known him as the quiet tagalong among the guys. But now, for some reason, you couldn't keep the girls off him. Even Jason couldn't explain it.

Suddenly, Cedric heard a commotion from the opposite

end of the parking lot, near the club entrance. He walked over to see what was up.

There were J-Wahl and their other bud practically buried under a pile of guys, every one of them out for blood, punching and pounding Jason and his friend. Cedric tried to count the flailing arms and furious faces. There must have been about thirty of them, all wailing on the two guys from Laguna Beach. He knew Jason could take care of himself in a fight. Growing up as the youngest kid with older brothers, Jason had long since learned to defend himself, but this was crazy. This wasn't even close to a fair fight.

"Hey, man, knock it off," Cedric said, grabbing the closest guy and trying to pull him off his buddies. A fist came out of nowhere and clocked him. Then another. Cedric caught sight of Jason for a split second, swinging, one eye almost swollen shut, before he disappeared under the bodies.

"All right, break it up! Break it up!" a deep voice growled behind Cedric. Someone grabbed him by the back of his shirt and yanked him out of the fray. The noise had drawn the club's linebackerlike bouncers over, and they were prying the brawlers apart, most of them still swinging and swearing, until they'd separated the warring sides and calmed people down enough to send them off in opposite directions, away from club property.

As they limped back to their car, Jason bleeding and swearing under his breath, Cedric glanced at his friend. His face was already beginning to puff and swell from the innumerable punches.

"So, what happened, bro?" Cedric asked as he started the engine.

Jason shot him a sidelong glance. His lips were so swollen it was hard to understand him. "That kid looked at me funny," he mumbled. "He made a comment I didn't like."

"Wait, *you* started it?" Cedric asked incredulously. "Did you not see how many of them there were? What were you thinking?"

Jason shrugged and inspected his swollen face in the rearview mirror.

You had to admire the guy, thought Cedric as they drove away. J-Wahl was a tough kid. He didn't back down even when the odds were stacked against him.

# Cedric

## The Pitch

Cedric stood on the pitcher's mound staring down the batter. Never show emotion. Never let the batter know what you're thinking: His dad's words rang in his ears from years of baseball practice.

But the kid was crowding the plate, and Cedric was annoyed. He figured he'd throw a warning pitch to signal him to back off. He wound up and let the ball fly, high and inside. Before the batter could swing, the ball caught him on the left cheek. There was a sickening crunch, then the kid dropped the bat and crumpled to the ground, his hands over his face, his legs pulled up in agony. In seconds everyone from the catcher to the coach swarmed over the injured batter. Cedric could barely catch a glimpse of him through the crowd, but he saw enough to know that the kid's face was a mass of blood. His pitch had shattered the boy's cheekbone and dislodged his eye from the socket.

Never show emotion, he told himself as he stared in disbelief at the damage he'd caused, and heard the ambulance siren in the distance. He knew his dad meant well with the advice. But he was only twelve. Dad would let him slide just this once. He'd have to.

# Cedric
## The Science Class Incident

The bell hadn't yet rung to signal the start of seventh grade science class, and students were still wandering in, getting settled at their desks, pulling books and pens out of their bags. Cedric glanced up toward the clock at the front of the room to see just how much time he had left to hang out and talk with friends before class actually started. A kid in the hallway poked his head in the door, then darted away. A few seconds later, he did it again. He didn't even belong in this class. What was he doing? Curious, Cedric headed to the door of the classroom and peered out to see where the guy had gone. Without thinking, he slipped his hand around the edge of the doorframe to get a better grip as he leaned out of the room. Wham! The kid appeared from around the corner, charged toward the door, and slammed it shut as hard as he could. Cedric blinked down at his hand in disbelief. He couldn't feel any pain, but blood was spurting everywhere. His nearly severed fingers were dangling from his knuckles like something out of a horror movie.

Whoa! Cedric thought to himself, I'd better go to the office. He didn't wait for a permission slip from the teacher. He tore off in the direction of the principal's office, where the shaken staff packed his hands in ice and called 911.

Later that day, after a plastic surgeon reattached his fingers, Cedric got the good news that his hand would be back to normal in a few months. Still, he couldn't help wondering if it was some kind of karmic, cosmic payback from the baseball gods for shattering that batter's face earlier in the year.

# Cedric
## Serious As a Heart Attack

Cedric was just walking the family dog. No big deal. It wasn't like he'd run a marathon. So why was his chest killing him? He tugged on the dog's leash. "Hang on," he said, gasping. "Slow down a minute."

These were the sharpest, most intense pains he'd ever felt, and they were ripping right through his rib cage. What the hell was going on? He played baseball and skateboarded all the time and this never happened. It felt like he was having a heart attack. Could twelve-year-olds get heart attacks?

Clutching his chest with one hand and the leash with the other, he made for home as fast as he could.

"Mom, I don't feel so good," he said when he saw her. "My chest is killing me. I think there's something wrong with my heart."

"We'd better get you to the doctor right away," his mom said, looking alarmed.

"He'll be fine," his dad reassured her. "Just let him catch his breath."

Normally, Cedric admired his dad's toughness. You didn't go from having zero cash and living in your car while you struggled to pay for college to having a nice home in a place like Laguna Beach as Cedric's father had done, without being tough. But this time, he sided with his mom. Something intense was going on behind Cedric's rib cage and he wanted it to stop. The sooner the better.

A short time later, surrounded by medical charts and the smell of antiseptic, Cedric listened intently to the doctor.

"I'm going to make you faint," he said. "Don't worry. It won't hurt."

Cedric nodded hesitantly. "Okay."

The next thing he knew he was waking up. His mother was looking down at him, next to the doctor, that same alarmed expression on her face.

The good news was the problem could be fixed. The bad news was that when he'd fainted his heart had stopped. He was going to need a pacemaker.

Man, thought Cedric, hearing the news. First I smash a kid's face. Then I get my fingers almost cut off. What else could go wrong this year?

He sighed resolutely. "Go for it, doc," he said. Anything was better than having those pains in his chest again.

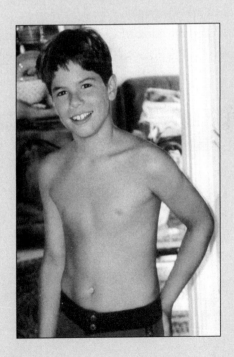

# Alex H.

## *Time Off*

Alex was starting to feel overwhelmed. Her bad grades from freshman year had been haunting her ever since, and now, only a month into junior year, her counselor was mapping out a schedule so crazy it made her head spin. In addition to the six regular classes she was already taking, she would have to earn extra credits by signing up for adult education history and math courses.

There was no way Alex was going to miss out on her senior year. No way she was going to miss out on graduating with all her friends. But there was also no way she could get all of this done. If she followed the counselor's advice, she would just about kill herself in the process. There had to be a different way to catch up.

Finally, she thought of one. She had always wanted to try homeschooling. Why not do it now? She ran the idea by her parents, her counselor, the school administration, and then the people she knew would take it the hardest: her friends.

Kristin, Morgan S., and Alex M., her closest girlfriends at the time, said they would miss her, but they promised not to lose touch. They vowed to see her every day and keep her up-to-date on all the gossip.

At first it felt weird going to the homeschool office downtown to get her books and assignments. There were no exams, no finals, no bells to signal the end of class, and no teachers to keep her in line. All the self-discipline had to come from Alex herself. She had to fight the urge to hang out at home all day watching soaps or talking on the phone, and then cram all the work in at the last minute. But eventually she settled into a routine of studying, doing her assignments, and taking them to the office three times a week to be graded. She couldn't believe she was getting all her work done and she still had time left over to do what she wanted. In fact, she had so much free time on her hands that she got a job at a local surf shop a month after starting homeschool.

Alex's friends stayed true to their word, calling or hanging out with her every day when their classes ended and bringing her along to all the parties. Seeing her girlfriends was the highlight of the day every day. (She would never have believed that, by next fall, she and Kristin would hardly be on speaking terms with Alex M.)

When spring finally rolled around, Alex snapped the cover shut on her last homeschool textbook and gathered up the last assignment she would ever need to turn in to the office downtown. The whole summer stretched out ahead of her invitingly. No night school. No summer classes. No need to panic about earning extra credit in the fall. She couldn't believe she had managed to catch up so easily.

No teenager actually wants summer vacation to end, but Alex came close. She couldn't wait to start her senior year. She knew she had enough self-discipline to study on her own, but it just wasn't the same. She wanted to be able to sit next to her friends in class again and look forward to Fridays like she used to. She wanted to hang out in the quad and gossip about who was hooking up and who was breaking up. She wanted to roll her eyes when the teachers droned on too long and suffer through pop quizzes and gripe about the dress code and hear the bell ring at the end of the day. She wanted to go back to school.

# CASEY

"He is too cute!" Casey said, nudging her friend Jenny and pointing out a boy competing in the skimboard contest they were watching on the beach near Casey's house. Blond hair, tan skin, great bod. And he looked like he was just about their age.

As they watched, the boy dropped his board onto the wet sand and hopped lightly on top of it. He glided out toward an oncoming wave, banked off it effortlessly, and then rode it gracefully back into shore. Casey thought he caught her eye once or twice, but maybe it was just her imagination.

When the contest ended, she admired him as he shook the water out of his hair, gathered up his board . . . and walked right over to where she and Jenny were sitting in the sand.

"How ya doin'?" he said. "I'm Sam."

Casey tried to act casual and friendly, though her heart was racing through the whole conversation. Sam, as it turned out, was exactly their age, about to start his senior year. Even better, he went to Laguna Beach High, where Casey was going to start school in the fall.

The decision to switch schools right before senior year hadn't been an easy one for Casey, but after her closest friend at her Christian school died during junior year, there were just too many sad memories to stick around. She needed a fresh start.

She wasn't sure how she would like public high school after spending most of her education in religious schools. But if all the boys looked like Sam it might turn out to be a smart move, she decided. When he asked for her phone number, Casey hoped she didn't look too eager as she scribbled it down and handed it to him on a scrap of folded paper.

"Great," he said. "I'll give you a call."

Casey and Jenny were still chattering about their new acquaintance a few hours later as they headed into one of their favorite Mexican restaurants for dinner.

"Oh no!" Casey squealed, ducking behind Jenny. "I don't believe it. There's Sam!" She had eaten at the restaurant countless times. How could she never have noticed a waiter as hot as Sam? After recovering from her initial embarrassed shyness, Casey asked to be seated in Sam's section. Soon they were chatting easily whenever he got a few minutes of downtime between customers.

Sam called Casey when he got off work and they made plans to meet at a skimboarding movie premiere at Hennessey's Tavern a few hours later. The premiere was filled with kids their age, and Sam knew everyone. He introduced her to so many of her future classmates that she soon lost track of names. She recognized one friend of his—a girl named Kristin—from freshman year at Santa Margarita, though they'd been in very different cliques.

The more time Casey spent with Sam, the sweeter and more charming he seemed. They saw each other almost every day for three weeks. The first day of school was right around the corner. How great would it be to start school having a gorgeous boyfriend like him? Everybody already referred to her as "Sam's new girlfriend."

Although when she thought about it, she wasn't sure most of them actually knew her name. What if they never thought of her as anything but Sam's girlfriend? People would probably assume she transferred to their school just to be with him. They might not even bother to get to know her.

Casey had gone to her share of different schools in the area, and she knew how tough it could be for a new girl to break in socially, especially in a place where cliques were old and established, where the kids had gone to school together ever since first grade. To make matters worse, senior year wasn't exactly prime time for forging friendships in any school. Maybe she'd be better off staying with Sam. But she had to give it a shot. She really needed to make some new friends, both guys and girls.

"I think we're better off just hanging out," she told Sam shortly before school started. "I don't want to have a boyfriend this year."

Sam took the news better than many of the girls she had met through him did when they found out. All of them adored Sam. They couldn't believe Casey would dump him. "Are you stupid?" they demanded. "He's the best guy in our school. What were you thinking?"

"It's all gonna be downhill from here," they warned.

# CASEY

## Movie Star

It was a catch-22. You couldn't act in movies if you didn't have your Screen Actors Guild card, and you couldn't get your Screen Actors Guild card if you hadn't acted in movies.

To Casey, who loved performing so much that her grandfather nicknamed her Movie Star, having a SAG card of her very own was the ultimate dream. She had to find a way around the problem.

Recognizing how much she enjoyed the spotlight, Casey's parents helped her land modeling jobs as a child and—even better—built her a stage room in their house where she could dress up and perform. For Casey and her friends, the room was a fantasy come true, stocked with sparkly dresses, gold boas, big glasses, and glamorous accessories. With Casey at the helm as choreographer, writer, director, and lead actress-singer-dancer, they put on countless shows for her family.

When she finally got the chance to audition for a role in a real movie called *Bernie and Bogie* during her freshman year, Casey prayed it would be the break she had been waiting for. It was just a small part, in which she would portray the film's child star at age sixteen, but it might be enough to get her that SAG card she had always dreamed of.

Casey did her best at the audition. Then she held her breath.

"She's perfect for it!" she overheard the casting director whisper. "She looks just like the star, only older."

She would have preferred to be noticed for her acting talent rather than her looks, but she'd take what she could get. And this sounded promising. Then the woman's next question dashed all her hopes.

"You have your SAG card, right?"

Casey shook her head. She waited for them to tell her thanks-but-no-thanks and shoo her out. Instead, the woman leaned over and whispered to the man seated next to her, then she turned back to Casey.

"Okay," she said cheerfully. "Come back next week when we start filming."

"WHAT?!"

The woman explained that because of Casey's striking resemblance to the star, they could apply for an exception to the Screen Actors Guild rules that would let her act even without being a member. Best of all, after this she would actually be able to get a SAG card!

Casey loved every moment of filming *Bernie and Bogie.* But that was nothing compared to the day when she opened the mail and found a letter welcoming her to the Screen Actors Guild along with her very own membership card.

She kept tucking the card into her wallet, then pulling it back out to make sure it was still there. Seeing it was the greatest feeling ever. True, it didn't quite earn her the nickname Movie Star, despite what her grandfather thought. But it was a step in the right direction.

# Alex M.

## *Older Men*

It was universally accepted among high school girls in Laguna Beach that boys their age were lame. If you had any brains, you'd date an older guy if you could get one.

Alex was no exception. She dated a senior when she was a freshman, and by the time she was a junior she was dating a college guy.

He was gorgeous and sweet and *so* much more mature than the guys her age, as she assured her girlfriends. High school boys were nothing compared to college men when it came to romance. On her birthday, Alex's boyfriend surprised

her by kicking his roommates out for the evening, making her a pasta dinner, and then filling the whole house with candles and playing their song as she walked in. When Alex told her friends about it, they practically turned green with envy. None of *their* boyfriends would do that.

So when her boyfriend dismissed junior prom as lame, Alex agreed. She was a little disappointed to miss out on shopping for a dress with the girls, going to the preparty, and riding in the stretch limo, but she didn't tell him how she felt. She had already made the mistake of going on spring break in Cabo without him, and they had gotten in an enormous fight as a result. She didn't need a repeat performance. Besides, Alex decided, she wouldn't want to make her boyfriend feel bad. She could see his viewpoint. For him, high school was over. Dunzo. When people asked if she was going to prom, she repeated what he had told her. "It's lame."

Instead, the night of prom she hung out with her boyfriend and his friends and wondered what she was missing. She couldn't help herself. She kept glancing at her watch. It was just about time for the preparty to start. Who would be wearing what? Would two girls commit the cardinal style sin of showing up in the same dress? Who would hook up? All her friends would be piling into the stretch limo for the ride to prom right about now. She pictured them craning their heads out the top, yelling and waving at strangers they passed on the street. Prom would be just about starting . . . just heating up . . . just winding down. She sighed wistfully and turned her attention back to her boyfriend.

She really loved him, but by the end of the summer they agreed to move on. Or back, in Alex's case. You only go through high school once. You might as well have some fun while you're there. Even if you'll think it's lame in a few years.

# LAUREN

## The Homecoming Princess Diaries

Ever since freshman year, Lauren had been dreaming about being named a homecoming princess. Now that she was a senior, this was her fourth year as a member of ASB, the student group in charge of planning dances, parties, and other school social activities including homecoming events. Along with the other freshman, sophomore, and junior girls in ASB, Lauren had helped organize kidnappings of newly named princesses every year, always hoping that one day her turn would come.

The kidnappings were a blast. The girls' parents would get so excited when they found out their daughters had been singled out by their classmates for the honor that they would eagerly take part in the ruse. They would pretend to know nothing, then rise early to unlock the doors for the underclassmen, who would barge in to kidnap the winners, waking them up with blow horns.

Hopeful senior girls all over Laguna Beach took care the night before kidnapping to dress in cute pajamas. Sometimes they would even get up at the crack of dawn to fix their hair and put on makeup so they could look good when they were whisked away to breakfast and presented with sparkly tiara T-shirts to be worn all day at school with those cute pajama bottoms. The best part of all was the ceremony at the homecoming game itself, where the five princesses walked out onto the fifty-yard line at halftime wearing their tiaras, their tuxedo-clad dads proudly serving as escorts.

The problem was, homecoming was just around the corner and Lauren knew she had no chance of being named to the court. ASB class members usually had a pretty good idea of who the year's princesses would be by this point, and Lauren had heard nothing to suggest her name might be among them.

So the evening before the kidnappings were to take place, she said good night to her parents and her younger sister and brother early, and headed up to bed. She thought about donning cute pajamas just in case, but decided it would depress her even more to wake up to nothing but the sound of the alarm clock dressed in special PJs. So instead she threw on an old pair of sweatpants and a ratty gray T-shirt. Someone had shrunk it in the wash so it didn't even fit anymore.

The next morning Lauren woke up bleary-eyed and confused. What was all that racket? It sounded like blow horns. Were there people in her room? She cracked one sleepy eye open and saw two beaming junior girls peering down at her.

"Is she awake?" one of them asked.

"Come on, Lauren!" the other shouted. "Get up! We've got to kidnap you!"

Lauren sat bolt upright, astonished, her grogginess gone in a second. "Are you kidding?" she nearly screamed. "Wait a minute! I need to change my clothes! I have some cute pajamas in my dresser!"

"No time!" the first girl said. "Let's go!"

Lauren grabbed a handful of makeup as they whisked her downstairs and out the front door. She caught a glimpse of her parents, her sister, and her brother, Brandon, all smiling broadly.

The whole day was a whirlwind. Lauren was so elated she didn't even care that she was wearing baggy old sweats while Lo and her other friends on the court strolled the halls looking adorable in their carefully chosen pajamas.

Once the idea that she wasn't dreaming settled in—she

really had been chosen for the homecoming court—Lauren realized she needed a dress to wear to the halftime ceremony. And not just any dress. For such a long-awaited and special occasion, she would need the perfect dress.

She shopped and shopped, but nothing seemed right. Finally, she spotted one with potential— a little black BCBG dress with a tight, tube-style top and a layered chiffon skirt that fell to midthigh and rippled gracefully when she walked. This just might be it, Lauren thought as she stood on tiptoe, turning this way and that in front of the dressing room mirror. But she had been on a strict clothing budget for as long as she could remember. She wasn't going to blow this amount unless she was sure it was *the* dress.

She stepped out of the dressing room barefoot and hurried over to the three-way mirror at the end of the row of changing rooms to get a better look at the dress from all angles. She was twirling right and left, admiring the effect of the rippling skirt when she heard a noise behind her. She turned around to see an older woman beaming at her.

"Oh, honey," the woman said. "That dress is beautiful. It dances, doesn't it?"

That was it. The sign she'd been looking for. How could you go wrong with a dress that danced? By the time Lauren got home and tried her new dress on again, she decided she liked it better than any other dress she had ever owned.

But just when things seemed to be going perfectly, her parents dropped a bomb at dinner that night. Lauren had forgotten all about the anniversary trip they were planning to take to Tahiti—right in the middle of homecoming week. Her dad would be gone. She'd be the only princess with no proud, tuxedo-clad father escorting her onto the football field for the halftime ceremony.

"We'll cancel the trip," her dad assured her, seeing how upset she looked.

"No," Lauren said. "You've been planning it for a year. The tickets are nonrefundable. And I know how much you and Mom have been looking forward to it."

"But what are you going to do?" her mom asked. "You can't walk out there alone. I'm sure your uncle would be happy to fill in."

Lauren shook her head. "That's okay. I'll think of something."

Just then Brandon walked into the room.

"Hey," said Lauren. "I've got an idea . . ."

Ten-year-old Brandon looked like a prince in his new tuxedo as he proudly escorted his sister to the fifty-yard line of Laguna

Beach High School's football stadium at halftime. And standing next to him in her dancing black dress, Lauren felt like a princess as she gazed up at the crowded bleachers.

When she got back home that night after it was all over, she placed her tiara carefully on top of her dresser. Come Monday, things would be back to normal at school. Anyone spotted in pajama bottoms would be sent home immediately for violating the dress code or forced to commit social suicide by wearing a gym uniform for the rest of the day. There would be homework and pop quizzes and gossip and all the other routine aspects of everyday high school life. But once in a while, if you were very lucky, you got to live out a fairy tale. At least for one night.

# LAUREN
## *Watercolors and Ice Cream*

Four-year-old Lauren dabbed her brush in the tin of watercolors and tried again to match the graceful lines and vivid colors of the pretty painting propped on the easel next to hers. She stood back to inspect her work. It still looked more like a messy orange blob than a bouquet of flowers.

"That's good," Diane assured her. "It's very good."

Lauren loved spending afternoons with Diane, the grandmotherly artist who lived next door to her family in Laguna Beach. She showed up every day after school, ready for an impromptu art or sewing lesson. Diane always answered the door with a smile, as happy to see Lauren as Lauren was to see her.

Lauren spent hours trying in her childish hand to copy Diane's graceful beach scenes and flowers while Diane patiently gave her painting tips, showing her how to blend the colors and apply them to the paper with delicate brushstrokes. Diane even bought Lauren a little sewing machine and helped her learn how to make clothes for her Barbie dolls.

When they weren't painting or sewing, the two of them would go downtown together to shop, visit the art supply store, or enjoy an ice cream cone. People often mistook them for grandmother and granddaughter, and that was fine with them. They thought of themselves that way, too.

Diane would often surprise Lauren by creating beautiful homemade Halloween costumes for her. One year it was a pink ballerina's tutu with lace and sparkles. Another, it was a mermaid's costume with a silver seashell top and a long green shimmery tail. Lauren wore it with a blond wig that reached all the way down to her knees. Years later she would still remember it as the best Halloween costume she ever wore.

For Lauren, who had recently gone from being the adored only child in the family to having a new baby sister, it felt wonderful to have an artist "grandma" to shower her with love, attention, and encouragement. "You're very talented," Diane would assure her. "Just keep practicing." Lauren promised she would.

So when Diane got sick a few years later, Lauren made sure she still visited as often as possible. She admired the way Diane simply switched to painting with her left hand when she could no longer use her right. Sometimes she'd hear Diane coughing when she knocked on the door. But she would always stop the moment she saw Lauren, ready to greet her with a smile and a cheerful hello.

After Diane passed away Lauren kept her promise, sketching out ideas for her own clothing designs on a notepad in the backseat of the car whenever the family took vacations and later doing renderings for her father, adding color, shading, and depth to the architectural sketches at his office. Lauren never stopped practicing and she never lost her passion for art and design. She knew that Diane, like any good grandmother, would have been proud of her.

# TALAN

*Yahoo!*

With a former model for a mom, it was no surprise that Talan had done a little modeling himself as a child. Whatever gene made you start singing and dancing when you saw a camera, he'd inherited it. Tucked away somewhere in the family archives there was a videotape of a pint-size Talan dancing around the house in tightie whities, belting out "Another One Bites the Dust" to prove it.

In first grade he'd even taken tap dance lessons and melted all the parents' hearts onstage at the school talent show by wearing a tiny tuxedo and top hat and dancing with a little girl classmate.

He wasn't quite that uninhibited these days. He'd sometimes sing for his closest female friends, but he made them turn out the light first so he'd be less embarrassed.

Especially when he sang for Taylor. There was something about that girl. Even though they were close friends and knew everything about each other, including all of each other's flaws, she was unlike any other girl. Talan still remembered the day he'd met her in seventh grade. She'd been hanging out with his friend Sam under the palapa at Ninth

Street Beach and Sam had introduced them. A few years later, Talan had told Taylor's mom he was going to grow up and marry her daughter.

Taylor and the other girls always assured him that he had a good voice. Why not sing if he wanted to? "Naw," Talan would say. Singing wasn't exactly number one on the list of cool-guy things to do in Laguna Beach.

Looking cool to your friends could rule your life in the Bubble if you weren't careful. Talan had even dropped off the football team freshman year because the popular kids considered football players meatheads. He missed it, though. And when his dad accused him of being too much of a wimp to go back, it was the last straw. He rejoined the team junior year.

Rediscovering his onetime favorite sport was making Talan think about other stuff he'd loved to do earlier on, before he'd cared what other people thought. He remembered that he had really loved performing.

"Mom, I think I want to act," he told her. Together they found an agent in the fall of Talan's junior year. But, following his mom and his new agent's advice, Talan tried not to get his hopes up too high. A lot of teenagers in Southern California dreamed about becoming performers. That didn't mean it was going to happen.

So Talan was as surprised as anyone when he landed a national commercial for Yahoo a short time later. When he drove to the set he was even more amazed to find a multimillion-dollar studio with bright lights everywhere and painters and set designers constantly adjusting colors. There must have been fifteen guys buzzing around just making sure all the equipment ran right. They even had a tutor on the set for him. He was blown away by the elaborateness and the excitement of it all.

He knew he had to find a way to do more acting, get more experience in front of a movie camera as soon as possible. But he was still in high school. How, he wondered, could anyone get that kind of experience without leaving Laguna Beach?

# LAUREN ANd LO

## An Announcement

ASB students almost always got the inside scoop on important school news before it reached everyone else. So when Lo knocked on Lauren's classroom door and asked the teacher if she could talk to Lauren in the hallway for a few minutes, Lauren knew something huge must be going on.

"What is it?" she asked, stepping out into the hall and closing the classroom door behind her. She hoped nothing serious had happened.

"MTV is coming here!" Lo burst out, barely able to contain her enthusiasm.

"Where?"

"HERE! To Laguna Beach High School. They're going to make a reality show about us!"

"Us?" Lauren repeated, confused.

"Yes!"

By noon the entire school would be buzzing with the incredible news. Lines of hopeful high school students would snake through the quad, waiting for their turn to fill out lengthy application forms. All anyone would talk about in or out of class during the upcoming weeks was how they had answered the questions on their applications, who they heard was getting callbacks for second auditions, and who might be among the lucky handful of students to be featured on the upcoming MTV show.

"You do realize that they're not going to include everyone from our school in the show, don't you?" Lauren asked Lo.

"I know," Lo replied breezily.

"But you said they were making a show about us."

Lo nodded.

"You meant us, as in Laguna Beach High School in general, right?"

"No, stinkface. *Us.* You. Me. All our friends."

"But what makes you think they'll pick us?"

Lo smiled. "I just know," she said. "It'll be us. Who else would it be?"

# Acknowledgments

Many thanks to Gary Auerbach, Dick Bosworth, Ellen Bosworth, Lo Bosworth, Jeff Boyle, Rick Boyle, Dennis Cavallari, Kristin Cavallari, Cedric Channels, Mitchellene Channels, Taylor Cole, Bruce Colletti, Lorilee Colletti, Stephen Colletti, Jim Conrad, Kathy Conrad, Lauren Conrad, Tony DiSanto, Adam DiVello, Liz Gateley, Karen Hogenauer, Alex Hooser, Eugene Hooser, Lisa Madsen, Caroline Pessoa Murphy, Alex Murrel, Annette Murrel, Craig Murrel, Kathryn Murrel, Jeff Olsen, Miki Olsen, Morgan Olsen, Judy Phillips, Stan Phillips, Trey Phillips, Casey Reinhardt, Kelly Roberts, Dieter Schmitz, Henry Schmitz, Pamela Schmitz, Christina Schuller, Donna Schuller, Robert Schuller, Darrell Smith, Jessica Smith, Karen Smith, Mary Souders, Morgan Souders, Scott Souders, Christy Spitzer, Charlene Torriero, Roger Torriero, Talan Torriero, Denese Wahler, Jason Wahler, and Rick Wahler.

As many as 1 in 3 Americans have HIV and don't know it.

# TAKE CONTROL.
# KNOW YOUR STATUS.
# GET TESTED.

To learn more about HIV testing, or get a free guide to HIV and other sexually transmitted diseases.

**www.knowhivaids.org**
**1-866-344-KNOW**

09620